FASHION *IN ACTION*

A series of concise, approachable books about current, global issues around fashion, offering readers guidance on how to become active participants in its future, and acting as calls to action.

SERIES EDITORS

Regina A. Root and Hazel Clark

BOOKS IN THE SERIES

Slow, by Hazel Clark
Appropriation, by Benjamin Linley Wild
Failure, by Nick Rees-Roberts
Animal, by Simona Segre-Reinach

APPROPRIATION

BENJAMIN LINLEY
WILD

BLOOMSBURY VISUAL ARTS
LONDON • NEW YORK • OXFORD • NEW DELHI • SYDNEY

BLOOMSBURY VISUAL ARTS
Bloomsbury Publishing Plc, 50 Bedford Square, London, WC1B 3DP, UK
Bloomsbury Publishing Inc, 1359 Broadway, New York, NY 10018, USA
Bloomsbury Publishing Ireland, 29 Earlsfort Terrace, Dublin 2, Ireland

BLOOMSBURY, BLOOMSBURY VISUAL ARTS and the Diana logo are trademarks of Bloomsbury Publishing Plc

First published in Great Britain 2026

Series design by Adriana Brioso
Cover image: Stephane Gagnon/Unsplash

A catalogue record for this book is available from the British Library.

A catalog record for this book is available from the Library of Congress.

ISBN: PB: 978-1-3502-5803-7
ePDF: 978-1-3502-5804-4
eBook: 978-1-3502-5805-1

Typeset by Integra Software Services Pvt. Ltd.
Printed and bound in India

For product safety related questions contact productsafety@bloomsbury.com.

To find out more about our authors and books visit www.bloomsbury.com and sign up for our newsletters.

CONTENTS

SERIES EDITORS' PREFACE

The *Fashion In Action* series responds directly to the upsurge of interest in critical issues in fashion—the industry, its ethics, its values, its contribution to global profits, its challenges amidst profound planetary change. When we choose what to wear, the connections we make might be understood as a chapter in a larger global fashion story. How do we re-imagine fashion as participants, encouraging a "freedom of thinking," while unraveling the past, challenging our present, and pointing to the future? This series goes beyond delineating global trends and fashion practices to imagine the very concepts of fashion anew. After all, we are planetary subjects in the making.

While appropriation in fashion has been a focus of considerable recent media attention, the same is not true of academic discourse. Benjamin Wild's original and insightful text is timely and essential. Drawing upon and merging scholarship from different fields of study, this book takes a much needed discussion beyond only *cultural* appropriation. Merging theories from different disciplines that often do not reflect on each other, Wild enables us to build upon and cross-reference these ideas. In the process of bringing together disparate positions and finding commonalities between them, *Appropriation* fills an important gap, allowing us to reflect more carefully on the messages and meanings of a critical fashion concept that might otherwise get overlooked.

This book explores this controversial topic from multiple angles, making space for the complexity and messiness involved. In the process, we encounter original perspectives, making this all the more accessible to a wide audience. Appropriation can be a deeply emotional issue grounded in the layers of history and, in fashion, it is not to be judged as either "right" or "wrong," but rather skillfully approached through nuanced discussions that enable readers to assess and make their own evaluations.

Uniquely, and helpfully, Wild focuses on the differences in degree of appropriation in fashion, not just in kind. This book frames its perspectives within a discussion of modernity in relation to capitalism, mass consumption and industrialization, as well as emphasizing the significance of colonialism to the power dynamics of the subject. Still today, many appropriation conversations that remain stuck in modernity serve to entrench ideas of power dynamics that favor a more traditional instead of global understanding of fashion. The author emphasizes the importance of acknowledging the origins of appropriative acts and the assumptions that underpin them as perpetuating essentialist thought. Wild advocates, therefore, the need to place appropriation within a larger chronological frame that permits historical reflection. The book untangles layers of history and, together with an ever expanding fashion register, opens up our shared understandings of how today's conception and conduct of appropriation in fashion have been framed by "western" prisms of thought, including the shared origins of modernity and coloniality.

Fashion In Action divides each book into three parts and concludes with A Call to Action. Beginning with "Where Have We Been?," Wild hones in on the importance of language in addressing appropriation. The fact that most debates on the subject have been conducted in English, often reinforces a modern and "western" dominance, centering on the concept of possession, defined by emotions that can fluctuate, and legislation, which is largely fixed. The author highlights and problematizes the question of appropriation versus appreciation, which has become an increasingly thorny one in fashion, due typically to its focus on the intentions of any given circumstance, rather than the consequences for its subjects.

The first section introduces the theoretical underpinnings of appropriation in fashion, including the work of a number of recent fashion studies scholars. The work of Angela Jansen, and her colleagues in the Research Collective on Decolonial Fashion (RCDF) among others, have proven especially revealing in their unpacking of decolonizing and decentering approaches of fashion studies in the academy, conceptualizing new instances of appropriation and the colonial dynamics that underscore them. Scholar Minh Ha Pham's concept of *racial plagiarism* is also introduced. Examining knockoff culture, Pham highlights and complicates the problematic nature of what is deemed "appropriation" through the perceived power dynamics between race, gender, and class. Wild explains that cultural appropriation is inescapable when cultures come into contact with one another as, inevitably, they do. He emphasizes how appropriative acts are a fundamental part of human culture, referencing Richard Rogers' concept of transculturation, to move the significance of appropriation from a culture's periphery to its center.

The importance of social media to this subject is highlighted, especially in the subsequent chapter, "Where Are We Now?" It serves as the major medium for fashion consumers (rather than scholars, journalists or industry professionals) to call out instances of appropriation. The book highlights how the academic scholarship it references needs to find more of a place in informing mainstream discussions on appropriation in fashion, which rely mostly on the media. While many of the theories and viewpoints summarized in the first chapter may be unfamiliar to readers, the accessible instances unpacked in the chapter that follows serve to illustrate them. They are presented as six recent "Episodes" of appropriation in the fashion system, which also attracted media attention. They demonstrate the many contrasting opinions about appropriation in fashion.

This book provides the opportunity of aligning public, media and academic discourses to comprehensively understand the issues involved. It highlights how multiple views of the phenomenon exist concurrently, resulting in markedly different assumptions about its acceptability. Much of the media reporting focuses on the immediate costs and benefits of appropriative acts, without reflection on the longer-term causes or implications, unless there appears to be a tangible impact for the business of fashion.

"Where Are We Going?." the last chapter, details the complexities of appropriation as both act and analysis. Approached through the concept of transculturation, appropriation is depicted as a defining part of culture, not just fashion. It reinforces the underlying premise of the book that this is a "knotty" subject, with cultural, emotional, intellectual, legal and linguistic complexities. Yet one of the final observations in this chapter is that the practice is also inevitable, and a fundamental part of human lives and cultures. Acknowledging appropriation as a social fact in need of nuanced discussion can, the book concludes, enhance understanding of the phenomenon. As new fashion imaginaries continue to emerge, new ways of thinking and being have the potential to inspire polyphonic dialogue. The final Call to Action draws upon the preceding chapters to challenge us as we gain fuller awareness, and thus avoidance, of appropriation in fashion.

Hazel Clark and Regina A. Root

ACKNOWLEDGMENTS

I am grateful to very many people who are helping me to challenge and develop my thinking on this topic; a project that remains ongoing. It is appropriate that I acknowledge the advice, scholarship, support, and patience of David Curtis-Ring, Angela Jansen, Ken Kweku Nimo, Mi Medrado, Samrat Prasai, Moses Turahirwa, Sarah Webb. Thank you to Regina Root, Hazel Clark, Frances Arnold, and the anonymous reviewers who commented on the completed text.

INTRODUCTION

To appropriate is to take something and make it your own, typically out of ignorance or in defiance of how it had existed before and who had previously owned it. Appropriation within the fashion industry is like "a riddle wrapped in a mystery inside an enigma," to repurpose (perhaps, to appropriate) the words of former British prime minister Winston Churchill.[1] On the one hand, novelty is an inherent characteristic of the anglophone concept of fashion. Since the nineteenth century, social commentators and theorists have argued that the pursuit of innovation and distinction is a major—even *the* primary—driver of new styles in human dress and appearance.[2] On the other hand, there is an equally long and compelling narrative within fashion reporting and dress history that argues these styles take inspiration from existing designs, so much so that "fashion copying is an ordinary part of the fashion business."[3] While innovation and appropriation are not necessarily opposing concepts, one of the chief reasons why fashions seem at once novel and familiar is because of the industry's tendency to emphasize new over old. André Leon Talley, a former creative director of American *Vogue*, and history graduate, explained the ambiguous place of the past within the fashion industry by invoking the shadow as a metaphor: "Fashion is not an industry that lives in the past, but rather carries its past along. Like a shadow, wherever it goes."[4] A disinclination to engage critically with history and to understand fashion's relationship with the past helps to explain why appropriation can occur and be largely overlooked. As myriad news stories about appropriation within fashionable designs demonstrate, the act is not consistently challenged even when the harm it causes, which can be economic, emotional, physical, spiritual, and any combination of these, is now widely communicated through social media.[5] This reticence is the same for appropriation that occurs between fashion brands and that which occurs between cultures, although the nature of the injury varies markedly; chiefly from specific and monetary in the former, to diffuse and psychological in the latter. The concept of cultural appropriation is more widely discussed in fashion journalism than the appropriation that occurs between brands, but both forms are considered in this book.

Within academic fashion studies discussions about appropriation, generally, and cultural appropriation, specifically, remain sparse. The situation is changing, and by its nature academic scholarship tends to acknowledge and respond to public behaviors and discussions only when they have existed long enough to become subject to sustained analysis. In 2024, fashion scholar Khémaïs Ben Lakhdar published *L'appropriation Culturelle: Histoire, domination et création: aux origins d'un pillage occidental*.[6] In three parts the book charts the development of largely academic thinking about the concept of cultural appropriation between the nineteenth century and present. Ben Lakhdar includes various examples from the contemporary fashion industry, although his analysis is rooted in his experience of living in France. In 2022, sociologists Yuniya Kawamura and Jung-Whan (Marc) de Jong published *Cultural Appropriation in Fashion and Entertainment*, although only one of the book's five chapters explicitly considers fashion.[7] The Cultural Authentication Process conceived by polymath Toyne V. Erekosima and fashion scholar Joanna B. Eicher in the early 1990s, cultural scholar Minh-Ha T. Pham's concept of racial plagiarism, articulated in 2017, and cultural scholar Serkan Delice's work on labor ethics, remain the only academic studies to specifically connect human dress and cultural appropriation.[8] The lack of written scholarly accounts on appropriation is likely also a consequence of the fact that much of the effort to call out and critique incidents of appropriation—cultural appropriation specifically—occurs online.[9] Instagram accounts like Diet Prada, founded in 2014 by Tony Liu and Lindsey Schuyer, have gained large numbers of followers (3.4 million as of July 2025) and a commensurate influence within the fashion industry for spotlighting the social and cultural transgressions of designers and brands.[10] Fashion scholars like Kimberly Jenkins have harnessed the internet to create the Fashion and Race Database, an "online platform filled with tools that expand the narrative of fashion history and challenge mis-representation within the fashion system."[11] Engaging in direct action to facilitate greater accountability and inclusivity within the fashion industry, Jenkins is also founder of the consultancy Artis Solomon, which "provides bespoke research and insight about fashion history and theory."[12] In 2019, she was hired to support Gucci's commitment to inclusivity following the brand's release of a sweater that was called out for its racist design.

In what follows, I cannot provide a comprehensive account of appropriation in fashion, but I do seek to introduce the major concepts and debates, so people can engage purposefully with the discussions that are taking place around this contentious topic. The main argument of the book is that the ahistorical outlook that facilitates appropriation in dress and appearance is a consequence of the fashion industry's "western"-centrism. I follow sociologist Yuniya Kawamura, who suggests fashion is a belief that "exists in people's minds."[13] I also agree with fashion scholars Linda Welters and Abby Lillethun, who contend that fashion is a global phenomenon, and a belief shared by people around the world.[14] Nonetheless, the belief of fashion that people possess is likely to be one that enshrines "western" values. At this juncture, it is important that I explain my positionality. I am a white British, cisgendered, nondisabled gay male. Much of my life has been spent in educational institutions. First as a pupil, where I was taught in single-sex schools, latterly as a student within a London university college, which describes itself as "one of England's oldest and most prestigious universities, founded within the tradition of the Church of England by King George IV and the Duke of Wellington who granted our royal charter in 1829."[15] I have since taught in secondary and higher education institutions within Britain. I am aware that my education and my subject, history, which remains a male-dominated discipline and does much (if inadvertently) to galvanize "western" thinking and values, is privileged and consequently peculiar. Through my work as an academic, which includes the writing of this book, I seek to challenge and learn beyond my upbringing, although I do not disavow it, nor do I presume to think that I can ever wholly overcome it.

Throughout, I place "west" between quotation marks because the noun is a concept and not a specific and unified geographical region. I also reject capitalization to avoid the suggestion that the concept should be invested with a singular status. Within the book the fashion that I reference is Fashion, a noun with a capital F. This connotes one of the world's largest, "western" industries that developed from the nineteenth century. I use Fashion in contradistinction to fashion, the verb, which refers to the practice of people, across divergent chronologies and cultures, who use their dress to frame their public identities.[16] These formatting choices are important because they emphasize the "western" focus that is inherent within the terms "fashion," and "appropriation." I consider the etymology of appropriation in Chapter 1. Here, I want to outline the concept's intellectual frame and its relationship to history, which is fundamental to understand why action is needed to better comprehend, and potentially combat, the causes and consequences of appropriation. Three factors need to be grappled with: modernity, colonialism, and race.[17]

A preoccupation with modernity is a peculiarly "western" phenomenon. Cultural scholar Elizabeth Wilson defines modernity as "oppositionalism and iconoclasm, [it is a] questioning of reality and perception, [it is an] attempt to come to grips with the nature of human experience in a mechanized 'unnatural' world."[18] An emphasis on mechanization is important because modernity is chiefly associated with the development of three factors that coalesced in Europe during the nineteenth century, where the origins of the concept as it is understood today are conventionally placed: capitalism, mass consumption, and industrialization. One of the key heralds of modernity was the establishment of what fashion scholars Caroline Evans and Alessandra Vaccari term "industrial time," which became globally standardized with the creation of Greenwich Meridian Time in 1884.[19] A concept of time that encompassed all people on Earth facilitated the efficiency and regularization that mechanization necessitated. It spurred the connectivity that consumption encouraged.[20] How Europeans adapted their values, their private and public behaviors to these seismic social facts adumbrates the condition of modernity.[21]

As Wilson suggests, modernity can be unsettling, destabilizing, wearying. According to philosopher Jürgen Habermas, this discomfiture encourages people to question socialized expectations of how they should act and behave.[22] Far from being a liberating experience, anthropologist Daniel Miller argues that the "pressure [on people] to create [their] own normativity . . . produces a tremendous desire for self-reassurance."[23] Consequently, to cope with the unnerving effects of "oppositionalism and iconoclasm," "western" people are likely to construct their realities in response to what they experience immediately and regularly, which seems certain.[24] Three linked consequences of this behavioral shift within the "west" are relevant to an understanding of why appropriation occurs. First, a focus on the present devalues the meaning and relevance of history, which appears to be the antithesis of contemporary preoccupations.[25] Second, by privileging the proximate and present, people are more likely to develop a unidimensional view of culture, which leads to the entrenchment of dominant "western" values.[26] Third, and a product of both, individual feelings of detachment and loneliness are likely to increase. Sociologist Norbert Elias suggests people may feel they have "an inner-self inaccessible to others."[27] A corollary of these attitudinal changes is that people become enmeshed in a frustrating search for belonging and connectivity, with themselves and others. Appropriation can appear to relieve these misgivings by acting as a psychological salve.

Literature scholars suggest that one of the reasons humans enjoy repetitions of the same stories is because of the comfort and structure these recitations provide:

> If we need narratives in order to give sense to our world, the shape of that sense is a fundamental carrier of the sense. Children know

> this when they insist on having familiar stories recited to them in exactly the same forms, not a word changed. If we need stories to make sense of our experience, we need the same stories over and over to reinforce the sense making. Such repetition perhaps reassures by the reencounter with the form that the narrative gives to life.[28]

On some level I think appropriation through dress acts in a similar way. Re-use of the same colors, materials, patterns, and shapes might be encouraged by mechanized garment-making processes to spur efficiency, but psychologically there is reassurance in encountering familiarity in dress, which is experienced intimately when we adorn our bodies, and because our clothes frequently become conduits for personal memories.[29]

Modernity's focus on the present and people's desire for reassurance also facilitates a specific form of appropriation: retro. Author Simon Reynolds defines retro as "a self-conscious fetish for period stylisation (in music, clothes, design) expressed creatively through pastiche and citation."[30] In the case of dress it "involves remaking and remodelling styles that were fashionable within living memory."[31] He argues that fashion facilitates retro revivals because its "relentless drive for constant change" means that garments retain a "use-value" long after their "symbolic value" has diminished.[32] Gifted or re-sold, garments can nonetheless reacquire symbolic value when they are worn in different circumstances. "An aura of uniqueness [can slip] back into the vintage garment" through an act of appropriation that "transforms yesteryear's mass-produced, mass-promoted trends into self-expression."[33]

The consolidation of European empires through an ongoing process of colonialism during the eighteenth and nineteenth centuries established modernity as a global concept, along with the "western"-centric qualms and behaviors it galvanized. In addition to many other self-legitimizing constructions that bolstered Europeans' pursuit of civilization—a word and concept largely invented during the nineteenth century—modernity justified "western" overseas interventions because it appeared to offer the linear, future-facing progression that had spurred European advancement to people deemed mentally and materially deficient. The reality was very different. The encapsulation of huge swathes of the world within prisms of "western" thought meant new definitions and modes of thinking were imposed upon colonies. If we consider that the British Empire—the largest to have ever existed—included 26 percent of the world's population by 1820, the impact of these shifts in thought is probably as hard to gauge as it is to overestimate.[34]

The histories of Europe's overseas subjects were especially vulnerable to spoilation because the "west" considered the past pliable. As new concepts—including civilization, homosexuality, heterosexuality—and disciplines—including geriatrics, sexology, statistics—were conceived during the nineteenth century to control

IMAGE 1 An example of retro clothing from an Old Navy & The Cut party during New York Fashion Week Party, 1994.
Source: Getty images.

the colonies, as much to protect European institutions and the ideas that underpinned them from overseas contamination, history was used strategically, certainly flexibly and dubiously, to support reassuring and valorizing narratives of "western" preeminence and progress. During the nineteenth century, history as a subject was nascent. It did not possess the criticality and objectivity that we now associate with the discipline.[35] An insightful, and frank, view of what history meant during this period is provided by English historian James Anthony Froude, who remarked,

> It seems to me as if history was like a child's box of letters with which we can spell any word we please. We have only to pick out such letters as we want, arrange them as we like, and say nothing about those which do not suit our purpose.[36]

Overseas cultures, which were almost always deemed inferior when compared with the "west," were treated very much like Froude's

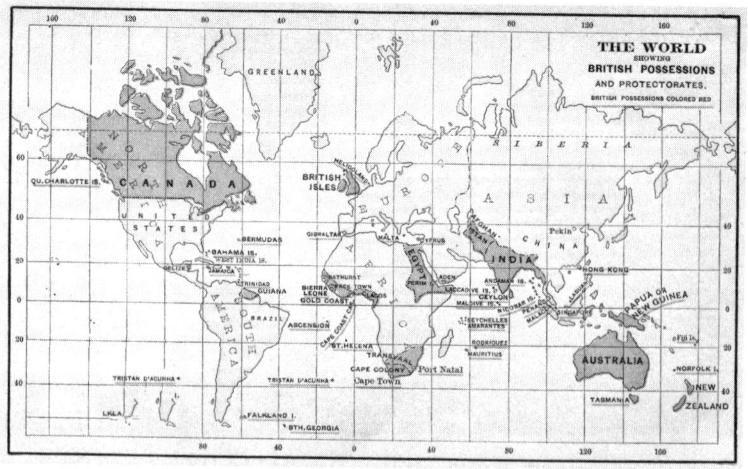

IMAGE 2 A map showing the extent of the British empire in 1883.
Source: Getty images.

letters. Consequently, their ideas, motifs, and objects were subject to fragmentation and appropriation by Europeans who sought to galvanize "western" values and behaviors. The ensuing Eurocentric narratives concretized "western" superiority and colonial subjugation, sparking a vicious cycle that made appropriation more permissible, more likely, and more unremarkable. Variations of these narratives continue to play out today, chiefly in the socialized binaries of age, gender, sex, and race that were defined in the crucible of empire.[37] Anthropologist David Graeber and comparative archaeologist David Wengrove suggest that arguments from the nineteenth century "never really ended; they keep resurfacing in different forms."[38] I contend that "[o]ne of the main [cultural] forms that continues to manifest these [ideas] is fashion."[39] The pliability of history is perhaps most evident through its contribution to definitions of race, as narratives of "western" people, their institutions and values were constructed to legitimize the ascendancy of all whites. Reinforced by empirical analysis, chiefly through the new discipline of anthropology, these histories meant whiteness became an important criterion upon which European perspectives were formed.

The importance of race within discussions of appropriation can be linked to shifting definitions of property. Legal scholar Cheryl Harris has argued that the racial characteristic of whiteness acquired a legal and cultural privilege similar to property because of the segregation and inequalities created and confirmed by colonialism and slavery. From the seventeenth century the status accorded to whiteness existed in contradistinction to blackness. This was because black people could be enslaved, white people could not. The status claimed by white people had important—drastic—implications for the concept of possession, which Pham describes as a "racial project."[40] Harris explains that

> [p]ossession—the act necessary to lay the basis for rights in property—was defined to include only the cultural practices of whites. This definition laid the foundation for the idea that

> whiteness—that which whites alone possess—is valuable and is property.[41]

To clarify how the codification and exercise of law within the "west" both elevated and protected white people, Harris cites a legal doctrine that established how they could be defamed if called black. A black person, however, could "not sue for defamation if [they were] called 'white.' Because the law expressed and reinforced the social hierarchy as it existed, it was presumed that no harm could flow from such a reversal."[42] The disavowal of black people was paralleled in the denial of their culture and property, which white people were, by implication, given sanction to appropriate. The legal and social subjugation of black people meant they were stigmatized, and legally prohibited, from doing likewise with white culture and property.

The racial project of property rights continues today. Reports of appropriation within the postmillennial fashion industry typically focus on trespasses that occur between cultures and involve a "western" designer or brand using motifs and materials without permission and acknowledgment from a non-"western" and other than white community. Several of these examples are considered in Chapter 2. The connection between property and race is so deep-seated that it is manifest in more diffuse forms. In her study of the ethical dilemmas caused and catalyzed by social media, Pham discusses the "Asian copycat formulation," in which it is presumed, chiefly by white people, that Asian fashion design is characterized by "imitation not inspiration."[43] "Western" commentary on Asian imitation is traceable to the seventeenth century, but the copycat formulation crystallized during the nineteenth century amid "western" fears about "Asian mechanicalness," which was apparently manifest in the "rote repetition and nonmeaningful or unthoughtful production" of Chinese and Japanese people.[44] During the twentieth and twenty-first centuries, the pace of economic and technological growth within the Asia-Pacific region meant centuries-long misgivings became blithely accepted as socialized fact, and a means of characterizing Asian people collectively.[45] The divisive rhetoric and policies against Asia and Asian

IMAGE 3 An Asian activist calling out Asian Hate during the COVID-19 pandemic.
Source: Getty images.

people that emanated from the White House during the presidency of Donald Trump between 2017 and 2021—particularly the insistence that COVID-19 was the "Chinese Virus"—is one such example.[46] The studies of Delice complicate discussion of cultural appropriation by considering how far people—specifically those outside the "west"—retain proprietorship of their labor, which has become increasingly devalued by transnational capital accumulation[47]

Modernity, colonialism, and race are increasingly challenged by academics and commentators for being constructs that, at best, impede human cooperation and development, and at worst, create circumstances and cultures that occlude them. Nonetheless, they remain challenging to tackle. Since the nineteenth century these concepts have simultaneously sanctioned "western" actions and assuaged the misgivings they have sparked. Consequently, their fixity, even imperceptibility, can make them appear intractable.

Appropriation is rooted in these constructs, as the above discussion has shown, and it, too, can be stubborn to critique. Recognizing this quandary, Pham declared the debate about cultural appropriation within fashion to be "pointless" in an article published in the American current affairs magazine *The Atlantic* in 2014.[48] Delice has said much the same, suggesting that the concept of cultural appropriation "at first sight, appears to be a mere empty signifier."[49]

In her article, Pham claims she is "getting tired of fashion criticism" because of "the predictable, limited, and unhelpful manner in which people talk about race in fashion."[50] Her fatigue derives from the "performance"-based nature of debates on cultural appropriation that focus on what has been taken and who is to blame for taking it, without fully considering the histories of the objects and ideas at the center of the furore, which typically reveal more complex narratives. The structure and tenor of current debates on cultural appropriation are consequently "pointless" in so far as they depend on reductive binaries—"high culture" and "low culture," and oftentimes, "first world" and "third world"—that preserve the hierarchical relations between the fashion industry and the cultures being appropriated.[51] Debates about cultural appropriation inadvertently galvanize the ideas and structures they seek to disrupt.

The chapters that follow are framed by Pham's rebuke. The differential impact of the COVID-19 pandemic, which has spurred calls for the fashion industry and fashion education to be more inclusive, make this an opportune moment to reflect on the current place of appropriation within fashion in order that we might take effective actions to better understand its causes and consequences, and to reduce the harm it can produce when confusion is created about an object's or a culture's origins and authenticity.[52] Chapter 1 considers where we have been. It examines the etymology of words associated with appropriation and critiques key theories that continue to frame discussions about these concepts within the fashion industry. This theoretical grounding facilitates the analysis of different examples of appropriation in Chapter 2, which focuses on where we are now.

Examination of the causes and consequences of appropriation for the fashion industry, fashion education, and consumers can help to identify key challenges within this contentious topic and, positively, present opportunities for overcoming the circularity of current appropriation debates noted by Pham. In conclusion, Chapter 3 draws upon the theories and case studies considered in the book to unravel the riddle of appropriation within fashion, at least to a sufficient degree to enable us to look to the future and consider how appropriation could, and should, be challenged and changed. Finally, and looking forward, Chapter 4 provides a series of prompts and propositions to spur a collective call for action.

1

WHERE HAVE WE BEEN?

The words people use and reject shape the creation, transmission, and impact of ideas. Khémaïs Ben Lakhdar points out that many of the words within mundane language usage in the "west" derive from cultures beyond Europe.[1] These words, jumbled into European sentences, raise broader questions about cultural inequalities, the thinking and behaviors they sanction. Language is especially important when thinking about appropriation because most debates about it are conducted in English, which reinforces "western" dominance.

Furthermore, the concept of possession, which has an especially strong resonance within the "west," is shaped by emotions, which can fluctuate, and legislation, which is largely fixed. Negotiating a topic that is expressed with equal validity through passionate and dispassionate language can easily create misunderstanding, offense, and intellectual cul-de-sacs where discussions have no clear means of resolution. All of this can hinder actions to comprehend and resolve tensions caused by cultural appropriation. Grappling with the conundrum of how to clearly and sensitively understand appropriation through the dominance of anglophone words and "western" concepts, this chapter reflects, first, on the genesis and interpretation of four words that are fundamental in ongoing discussions about the phenomenon: appropriation, cultural appropriation, cultural appreciation, and culture.[2] Second, I provide a critical introduction to the work of several scholars that can help to explain appropriation within fashion. While these choices reflect my thinking, the works considered are referenced within discussions about appropriation and provide an interdisciplinary perspective of the phenomenon. I focus on the writings of Minh-Ha T. Pham, Serkan

Delice, Yuniya Kawamura, Toyne Erekosima and Joanne Eicher, and Richard Rogers.

Appropriation is a beguilingly simple word. It describes a complicated action that can involve ideas and artifacts, physical and psychological violence, intense emotion. It can occur over a short or prolonged period, be explicit or subtle. It involves individuals and groups, local and international. The anglophone word derives from the Latin verb *appropriare* and noun *appropriationem*, which mean to take something as private property. The terms are first recorded in legal scenarios in late fourteenth-century England and document people's attempts to assert a singular authority over specific physical assets, chiefly property.[3] They do not appear in conjunction with art, and the taking of people's ideas, until the late nineteenth century.[4] The concept's expansion to include intellectual property meant more people could claim to be affected by appropriation, as both perpetrators and plaintiffs. By degrees, this development made any act of appropriation harder to define, its causes and consequences more complicated to identify.

The shift in meaning between the fourteenth and nineteenth centuries can be linked directly to the development of print, the emergence of a modern art market, and the increased commercialization of "western" society that fueled both. As the number and range of platforms that enabled people to express their creative and intellectual viewpoints increased, so did concerns about asserting ownership over them.[5] Within the fashion industry, concerns over appropriation are acute because clothing designs are not, for the most part, protected by copyright law.[6] While designers may apply individual and house styles to their creations, fundamental elements of human dress—a collar, a pair of socks, a derby shoe, an A-line skirt, etc.—could never be effectively copyrighted because of their universality. Another factor, which has come to assume greater importance in discussions about appropriation, is the expansion of Europe's overseas empires. During the eighteenth and nineteenth centuries, exchanges between Europeans and their colonial subjects were more heavily structured, even censured, by "western" governments and their representatives. The increasing importance of the colonies to European countries—economically, politically, socially—spurred debates that examined the potential and pitfalls of taking both artifacts and ideas from their international subjects. The significance of these discussions led, eventually, to the coinage of the compound noun "cultural appropriation."

The meaning of cultural appropriation is particularly complicated. In the strictest sense, the phrase describes the taking of artifacts and ideas from one culture and their incorporation into another. This dispassionate assemblage of words poorly conveys the emotional force of the actions they can label.[7] Cultural appropriation is first recorded in a published anglophone text of 1945.[8] The term was not widely used before the twenty-first century. The *Oxford English Dictionary* identifies only one other usage of it in the twentieth century, within an art book published in 1968. In its first recorded appearance, cultural appropriation refers to an unequal relationship between the cultures of Europe and Asia, where the former is assumed dominant.[9] In its second known usage, the term describes the economic reward that white people derived using black people's artistic and creative talents.[10] The circumstances in which the phrase initially appears hint at the volatility of the actions, and associated assumptions, that it defines. Google's Ngram Viewer, which records the annual frequency of word usage in published texts of various languages between 1500 and 2019, shows that transmission of the term "cultural appropriation" spiked in the late twentieth century. While the search facility is partial because it gives preference to European words, it is useful for highlighting that usage of appropriation has been on an almost vertical trajectory since the new Millennium. Prior to this, the word was hardly used.[11] This is an important point because the absence of a defining word or concept does not mean the noun or verb did not exist before. There are many examples of fashionable designs from the nineteenth and early twentieth centuries that would probably now be described as cultural appropriation even though their contemporaries would not have responded to them in this way.

For example, a recent exhibition within my local art gallery in Manchester, UK, included a black silk evening dress by French couturier Paul Poiret from autumn/winter 1921/1922. The object label placed the dress in its historical context and acknowledged that it would have been experienced very differently in the eighteenth century to today:

> [Poiret's] work often included silhouettes and decorative designs that referenced styles from various cultures. We now acknowledge that this is cultural appropriation, the inappropriate or unacknowledged use of elements of a culture or identity that is different to one's own.[12]

Like many "western" artists and designers during the late nineteenth and early twentieth centuries, Poiret was inspired by an imagined view of cultures beyond Europe, which were fantasized and exoticized.[13] The costume designs of Léon Bakst for Sergei Diaghilev's *Ballets Russes* were hugely influential for "western" designers like Poiret, who hosted a fancy dress costume ball in 1911 called The Thousand and Second Night. The name was a play on the Middle Eastern folktales that are generally known in English as *One Thousand and One Nights*, or *Arabian Nights*. The name of Poiret's ball was directly influenced by the title of a short story by American author Edgar Allan Poe published in 1845. The influence of Bakst has persisted across centuries. It inspired Yves Saint Laurent, who produced a collection called Opéras—Ballets Russes in 1976. It is also apparent in Dior's fall 2015 collection designed by Raf Simons.[14] More generally, "western" interest in an exoticized Middle East is evident in Alexander McQueen's womenswear collection for spring/summer 2000, Eye which featured crescent moon and star motifs, gilt embroidery, and elongated eye make-up.[15]

Today, designers and fashion brands might be more cautious, more aware of what might be considered blatant cultural copying. Nonetheless, the increased usage of the term "cultural appropriation" since the new Millennium, coupled with the fact that an anglophone phrase is used to label an ambiguous and emotionally charged action that is synonymous with superordinate white "western" people taking from subordinate non-white and non-"western" people, is problematic.

The coinage of cultural appropriation in the twentieth century coincided with the end of the Second World War and the beginnings of decolonization, a process by which European countries, initially Great Britain, ceded governmental authority of their overseas colonies to indigenous populations, giving them political independence.[16] The marked increase in the term's usage during the twenty-first century correlates with the launch of social media platforms, which have become one of the chief mediums for people to spotlight and critique perceived infractions of appropriation, particularly within the "western" fashion industry: Facebook launched in 2004; Twitter (now X), in 2006; Instagram, in 2010. The emphasis on the "west" is important because social media engagement tends to be greater within wealthier countries.[17] This may inadvertently prioritize "western"-centric judgments in discussions about cultural appropriation. Increased usage of the term certainly aligns with growing concerns, largely from within the "west," about the inequalities that globalization and the attendant spread of "western" values has caused to the detriment of regional identities and experiences. Such concerns were catalyzed by the differential impact of the COVID-19 pandemic between 2020 and 2022 and the regalvanization of the Black Lives Matter movement. Consequently, while cultural appropriation might appear to be a neutral, purely descriptive phrase, its conception and continued usage prioritizes a "western" perspective.

The term's current utility supports cultural scholar Minh-Ha T. Pham's assertion that property rights constitute a "racial project."[18] These circumstances do not necessarily invalidate the term, but cultural appropriation does not occur without at least two parties, and its causes

IMAGE 4 An early twentieth-century fashion plate depicting a woman wearing a Persian turban.
Source: Getty images.

and consequences cannot be effectively understood if the views of just one are given preference or considered alone. This is especially the case when the views of the perceived transgressor are prioritized. As we have seen, this is another criticism of discussions about cultural appropriation made by Pham.[19] The situation might be changing. Cultural

IMAGE 5 A model wearing an ensemble from Yves Saint Laurent's Fall 1976 couture collection.
Source: Getty images.

scholar Serkan Delice has demonstrated how the concept of cultural appropriation is increasingly used—perhaps appropriated—by artisans outside the "west" as a critical tool to understand and defy "capital's hierarchical segregationist divisions of labor and its dispossession of the many of their productive forces for the benefits of the few."[20] They deploy the term to emphasize the negative consequences of appropriative acts that objectify their labor.

In current debates about appropriation, cultural appreciation is conventionally perceived as the binary opposite to cultural appropriation. Cultural appreciation can refer to acts of appropriation that involve the source culture and its people as willing collaborators. It can also refer to appropriation where the copyist seeks to celebrate and show respect for another culture.[21] The reality is more complicated. First, cultural appropriation and cultural appreciation are not antonyms; in language or deed they do not exist at opposite ends of a figurative scale. Google's Ngram Viewer indicates that the term "cultural appreciation" has circulated in anglophone texts since at least 1900. There were peaks in its usage in 1936 and 1983, long before its supposed opposite term "cultural appropriation" became widespread during the twenty-first century.[22] Pham challenges the use of cultural appropriation and appreciation on the grounds that they are euphemistic.[23] When the terms are used together as some kind of intellectual toxin and antitoxin, she suggests the causes and consequences of these phenomena are obscured. A focus on individual experiences that are variable and often passionate obscures understanding of the relationships of power that influence appropriation and that typically privilege "western" perceptions and priorities.[24] Most scholars would probably accept as fiction—one pleasant for the "west"—that cultural appreciation can be positive. Any white "westerner" who asserts the value of the term is likely demonstrating their "white innocence." The phrase is a coinage by English scholar Ayanna Thompson that seeks to encapsulate how white people invoke an apparent ignorance about the racial hurt they cause to exonerate and reprieve themselves from confronting their behavior and values.[25]

The "western" partiality of the terms "cultural appropriation" and "cultural appreciation" is emphasized if we consider the noun culture. The etymology of culture derives from French and Latin sources. In the fifteenth century, when the Latin word *cultura* first appears in a published text, it describes the prosaic act of preparing soil for crops.[26] The association with edification and the cultivation of the human mind, which moves us closer to present-day understandings of the term, appears to have originated in the sixteenth century. During the seventeenth century this meaning became commonplace among an anglophone readership. The earliest recorded use of the word "culture" to describe the customs and objects associated with a specific group of people occurs in history books published in the late nineteenth century. The first book, from 1860, is about slavery; the second, from 1867, is an account of the Norman Conquest of England.[27]

The shift in the word's meaning, from a definition of labor to something more abstract and related to learning, is attributable to a period in European history known as the Enlightenment. This was a time when empirical study, logic, and reasoning were lauded as both the preeminent methods of intellectual enquiry and the preferred traits of aspirant gentlemen; a focus on men reflected contemporary gender inequalities. During the nineteenth century a preoccupation with culture to distinguish groups of people was also important to justify European imperialism. Asserting the authority and legitimacy of "western" and white culture, in contradistinction to the barbarism and savagery of people beyond its borders, vindicated the global imposition of European values and practices in the colonies.[28] Academic Raymond Williams observes that many anglophone words became invested with new meanings during the nineteenth century—including "art," "class," "intellectual," "capitalism"—in response to the social, economic, and political changes that occurred in Europe during this period.[29]

Google's Ngram Viewer shows that usage of the word "culture" in published texts increased during the nineteenth century and still more during the twentieth century.[30] At the beginning of the new

Millennium usage began to trail off. It appeared to plateau in 2019, at which point the Ngram data currently stops. The decline in published appearances of the word "culture" could be apparent rather than actual, a consequence of how information for Google's Ngram Viewer is gathered. Declining usage may also reflect growing concerns that the term is negatively freighted because of its association with "western" priorities, which it can appear to legitimate and reinforce.[31] In addition to this historical baggage, pinpointing exactly what culture means is not straightforward because various definitions, each with different emphases, exist.

Two views of culture are dominant within academic literature. The first is explained by philosophers James O. Young and Conrad G. Brunk in their edited book *The Ethics of Cultural Appropriation*. They suggest that culture refers to a community's commonly held, if largely unselfconscious, ideas and values. Referring to the work of philosopher Ludwig Wittgenstein, specifically his example of a notional game, they explain how the constituents of something can be understood by many people, even if a precise definition remains elusive.[32] For example, the games people play have different rules and objectives, but they share many characteristics and can be readily conceptualized. The same is true for human culture. Myriad cultures exist throughout the world, but they are alike in having similar characteristics, typically relating to how individuals perceive themselves and treat others.

A second interpretation of culture is explained by academics Bruce Ziff and Pratima V. Rao, editors of *Borrowed Power: Essays on Cultural Appropriation*, who discuss a "western" tendency to view culture as "some type of creative product (whether tangible or otherwise)."[33] In this explanation, emphasis shifts from the beliefs people share to the "cultural goods" that make beliefs readily comprehensible. Examples conventionally include art, literature, film, music, theater, and dress. A focus on cultural products can result in artifacts and experiences being classified as "high" or "low." These binary classifications are loose, typically associated with class and taste, which can be equally treacherous to define, and contingent upon different communities and chronologies. High cultural products may be deliberately limited in number and scope because they require people to possess certain skills, experiences, or resources to access them. Consequently, they may be valorized for demonstrating the unique achievements of their respective community. By contrast, cultural products described as low are generally widely available. For this reason, they may be disdained for being ubiquitous or for presenting a view of their community that is mundane. Viewing cultural products hierarchically can also lead to broad classifications where prolonged periods of time are deemed to be "pinnacles of culture," to use the phrase of literature scholar Martin Puchner, or, in the case of the Middle Ages, merely a passing phase before Europe's rediscovery of classical learning during the Renaissance.[34]

On a superficial level, reference to cultural products facilitates consideration of appropriation because the ability to identify creators and owners can support the attribution of belonging and, where necessary, theft. In practice, discussion of products complicates the ascription of ownership. In its initial coinage, appropriation related to property that individuals and communities wanted to secure for themselves. While the ensuing legalities could be protracted, determining rightful ownership of a physical asset—a house, a field, etc.—was possible, and provable. However, as the meaning of appropriation has shifted to define something more abstract, including ideas and values, and in the case of cultural appropriation typically involves large communities of people with diverse histories, the delineation of belonging has become trickier.

Young and Brunk emphasize the challenge of establishing whether a culture can possess something, although their analysis assumes that this is possible, even for ideas and values.[35] Puchner rejects this premise. He argues that it is constraining, even inaccurate, to treat culture like property.[36] Many of the historical examples considered in his book, *Culture: A New World History*, which include stories from Egypt, India, Iraq, and Mexico, suggest the idea of owning culture is a "western" peculiarity. This is a reasonable assertion, considering the terms culture and cultural appropriation were conceived within the "west" and have contemporary meanings that reflect social facts from an avowedly "western" perspective. Instead, Puchner advocates for "cultural relativism."[37] This involves the acknowledgment, and appreciation, that culture is expressed in myriad ways, includes the tangible and intangible, and that any one culture or cultural product does not derive significance through its equivalence or ranking to another. The emphasis that Puchner gives to variation over resemblance elides with cultural theorist Homi K. Bhabha's conception of culture.

Bhabha's inclination to emphasize divergence when thinking about culture derives from his perspective as an Indian-English person. His early childhood was "caught on the crossroads that marked the end of Empire" and imbued with the multiple, complicated, and contradictory feelings this stirred.[38] He observes that a focus on difference highlights boundaries, or "in-between" spaces. These sites "initiate new signs of identity, and innovative sites of collaboration, and contestation, in the act of defining the idea of society itself" because of the negotiations sparked by the "overlap and displacement of domains of difference."[39] Fundamental to these processes is Bhabha's concept of hybridity, which asserts that all identities—individual and corporate—are formed from a mixture of different cultures.[40] He explains that the "enunciation of cultural difference problematizes the binary division of past and present, tradition and modernity, at the level of cultural representation and its authoritative address."[41] Consequently, hybridity challenges Eurocentrism and the dominance of "western" attitudes and makes it possible to "redescribe our cultural contemporaneity; to reinscribe our human, historic commonality."[42] Hybridity also challenges the "western" conception of possession, and with this the meaning of appropriation.

The preceding discussion has demonstrated how the words "appropriation," "cultural appropriation," "cultural appreciation," and "culture" can confound as much as clarify discussions about the concepts they describe. The terms are freighted with baggage that orientate them to prioritize a "western" perspective. This is important to keep in mind when thinking about appropriation in fashion because the fashion industry is frequently considered to be complicit, even a leading player, within the "west's" "project of modern civilization [that] has reduced cultures, nature and history to a pool of resources to be classified, extracted, and consumed," in the words of de-colonial scholar Angela Jansen.[43] Jansen's view, which is now vocalized with greater clarity, volume, and urgency following the COVID-19 pandemic, may explain why critical academic engagement with appropriation in fashion appears inversely proportionate to the frequency with which transgressions are reported within the media and news. While some academics have been active online and in advocacy roles for the industry's largest brands, raising awareness of appropriation and spurring practical measures to prevent it, prior to 2020 the fashion industry may have appeared to be too closely imbricated within the "west's" "project of modern civilization" to become an obvious, or straightforward, subject for the critical study of appropriation. Fashion scholars Rosie Findlay and Johannes Reponen consider how far fashion journalism, which has a significant role in shaping people's understanding of fashion and constitutes an important source for fashion criticism, exists "simply [as] a cheerleader for the fashion industry, complicit in circulating consumptive (and other) ideologies to audiences."[44] There are certainly cases where leading fashion journalists and fashion publications have expunged uncomfortable information because of public criticism. For example, in its report of Burberry's 2019 autumn/winter ready-to-wear collection Tempest, *Vogue*'s gallery of catwalk images omitted three looks that had been criticized for glamorizing suicide. Journalist Sarah Mower's accompanying commentary made no reference to the offending items.[45] Practices like this, even if not widespread, stymy effective criticism about the place and effect of fashion within a global society. For example, within Latin America, Caliban, a character within William Shakespeare's play *The Tempest*, has long been used to represent the monstrosity of Europeans and Americans. This demonstrates the myriad possibilities for interpreting fashion and the danger of regarding a "western" viewpoint as a form of norm or standard.[46]

Consequently, the discussions that ensue from censorship and distortion are more likely to be cursory and involve binary judgments along the lines of "good" or "bad," "right" or "wrong," which Pham suggests characterize current discussions about appropriation.[47] Another reason discussions about appropriation lack nuance is because there are few sustained considerations of the phenomenon within fashion studies, which as a relatively new field remains undertheorized. The four approaches reviewed below demonstrate that attempts are being made to understand the causes and consequences of appropriation within fashion, but their intellectual genesis is to varying degrees siloed because of their authors' professional and personal foci.

Theories of Appropriation (in Fashion)

Many studies consider the causes and consequences of appropriation and cultural appropriation in art, film, literature, and music. The methodologies used and conclusions reached within these works can be applied to fashion studies, which is inherently interdisciplinary, but sustained analysis of appropriation within fashion, and human dress broadly, remain limited. The following discussion provides a critical introduction to some of the more pertinent theories about appropriation and cultural appropriation, starting with those that focus on fashion and dress before casting the net widely to consider complementary theories from other disciplines.

To break the "deadlocked battle" between cultural appropriation and cultural appreciation in discussions of contemporary fashions, Minh-Ha T. Pham has made two suggestions that seek to emphasize facts over feelings in an effort to make discussions about these phenomena analytical and more purposeful. In so doing, she foregrounds the dynamics of authorship and authority, which are typically obscured by a focus on "western" designers and consumers. In 2014, Pham advocated for an "inappropriate" discourse to highlight the ideas and items that are not, and possibly cannot be, assimilated within "western" culture.[48] By asking what is not "appropriate-able," and what will not "continue to maintain the existing power structure of high fashion," she contends that it is possible to challenge the perception that the "west" possesses a monopoly on "how the world sees and talks about fashion."[49] For example, she suggests an "inappropriate" idea would be the assertion that a non-European country like Indonesia is capable of being the "self-aware originator of a fashion trend, rather than simply the third-world site for manufacturing cheap commodities."[50]

An inappropriate discourse expands analysis of fashion beyond the "west." Implicitly, it calls for commentators and scholars to develop their critical understanding of global cultures and histories if they are to accurately and sensitively identify what and why something cannot be appropriated from a non-"western" culture. Khémaïs Ben Lakhdar supports Pham's argument because he believes it leads to a dehierarchization (*déhiérchisation*) regarding who is able to create an item of fashion.[51] However, while we might assume that an increase in knowledge about different cultures could lead to a decrease in cases of cultural appropriation, the tenor of current discussions about the phenomenon, reviewed in Chapter 2, suggest this scenario is not immediately likely. Moreover, the concept of an "inappropriate" discourse was revised by Pham three years later.

Pham developed elements of her argument in an academic paper of 2017 that articulated the concept of racial plagiarism. The term describes an unsanctioned but legal copying from a designer or community of people who are other than white by a designer who is white. While a legal precarity exists for many "western" designers and brands because design works are not wholly protected by copyright, Pham argues that any criminalization of a copyist is determined "by social and economic power," which is typically weighted in favor of white people.[52] According to Pham, "The difference in the labeling of one act of unauthorized fashion copying as cultural appropriation/appreciation and another as a knockoff (or similar pejorative term) is the difference that race, gender, and class make in these determinations."[53] Consequently, discussions that dwell on the extent to which an act of appropriation is "good" or "bad" tend to reinforce the socialized thinking they seek to overturn.[54] White designers, who are preponderant within the fashion industry, can act with impunity without enduring the stigma of being labeled a copyist, knockoff artist, or design pirate.[55] Racial plagiarism is conceived to spotlight the exploitation and inherent inequalities that exist within acts of fashion copying. Pham highlights three points. First, acts of unsanctioned reproduction are never about appreciation. They will always deprive people of authorial control and denigrate their culture through a process that seeks to make it congruent, and acceptable to a dominant culture, which is typically "western" and white.[56] For Pham, this demonstrates the persistence of a colonialist attitude because other than white people, their cultures are seen as "natural, raw materials" that can be freely taken from.[57] Second, unauthorized appropriation "shuts out" other than white people. Denied their authorial agency, they are denied the right to capitalize on their experiences and resources. They are also removed from their histories, which cannot be freely explored and expressed.[58] The individual and communal voices of other than white people are silenced such that their contribution to dominant values and patterns of thought becomes nugatory.[59] Third, and connecting both points, racial plagiarism emphasizes how acts of appropriation are always, and obviously, political.[60]

Recently coined, the concept of racial plagiarism has not been widely adopted. It is referenced by cultural scholar Serkan Delice, whose work on cultural appropriation most readily aligns with Pham's focus on labor ethics. Nonetheless, a key point of difference between the two scholars is that Delice emphasizes transnational capital rather than colonialism in the framing of his research.[61] Two factors may preclude usage of Pham's term. First, it is presented as an alternative to cultural appropriation and cultural appreciation. While racial plagiarism can be adapted, it does not provide an analysis of appropriation that occurs between fashion brands. Second, the concept has a singular focus on race. An awareness that the causes and effects of appropriation are not always racially framed forms an important part of the argument made by Delice and sociologists Yuniya Kawamura and Jung-Whan (Marc) de Jong in their studies of appropriation and fashion.

Much like Pham, Serkan Delice argues that current discussions about cultural appropriation do not sufficiently consider the negative impact of appropriative acts on artisans' and craftspeople's labor, which has become devalued because of capitalism's prioritization of mechanized labor.[62] He suggests the marginalization of labor considerations in appropriation debates is a consequence of their eclipse by strongly asserted claims of cultural possession, which are typically conveyed "in the volatile, reactive space of social media."[63] Forceful and persuasive as these claims appear, Delice nonetheless suggests they are exacerbated by appropriative acts, rather than caused by them. Defensive claims to cultural ownership are symptomatic of the graver ills caused by the "dispossession" and "exploitation" of labor that forms part of "today's egregiously unfair transnational capital accumulation" alongside "the material and psychological legacies of colonialism."[64] Framed by Karl Marx's and Friedrich Engels' writings on living labor and anthropologist David Harvey's concept of accumulation by dispossession, which considers the commodification and "deterritorialising effects of contemporary capitalism" on culture, creativity and labor, Delice shows how people living outside the "west" use the concept of (cultural) appropriation to demand "unequivocal, and clearly acknowledged and compensated, involvement in the production of [fashionable garments]."[65] These assertions are made over claims of cultural copying, disrespect, and stereotyping, which tend to be the focus of most discussions of appropriation in fashion within the "west."[66] Consequently, a critique of appropriation, first, challenges the disrupting, disenfranchising consequences of globalization and, second, becomes a means to assert the necessity of design and manufacture, and the agency of people involved in these processes.[67] In so doing, it champions a more concrete view of culture that might enable it to be understood and enacted "as liberating practice in the face of capital accumulation."[68]

The contribution Delice makes to discussions of appropriation in fashion is important. He emphasizes the complicated, and fundamental, connection between capitalism, labor, and culture that facilitate the phenomenon, which no other scholar does, save Pham, and only to some degree. Nonetheless, however important capitalist behaviors and structures are in making appropriative acts more likely, we should probably be weary of downplaying the emotional response to them, which his remark about social media appears to do. His studies make it clear that appropriative acts impact people unequally as designers, makers, consumers. Delice's focus on labor helps to clarify the negative impact of appropriation on designers and makers, but there remains a need to consider these individuals and groups in parallel with others, not least consumers, who typically initiate discussions of appropriation. This is especially pertinent if his clarion call to use culture as liberating practice to challenge the dispossessions caused by capitalism is to be realized.

Yuniya Kawamura and Jung-Whan (Marc) de Jong examine cultural appropriation in fashion alongside entertainment, which they subcategorize as music, social media, television, and celebrity culture, largely drawing upon South Korean examples. Studies of cultural appropriation frame their analysis but they tend to regard the phenomenon solely as a "problem" that is "culturally offensive," "insensitive," and the cause of "intense debates."[69] These debates amount to a "hysteria" that stymies effective understanding, largely because they emphasize race.[70] Racialized infractions have been numerous within the post-Millennial fashion industry, but Kawamura and de Jong stress the frequency with which appropriations relating to religion and class also occur.[71] To comprehend and critique the variety of appropriations that have appeared within the fashion industry since the late twentieth century, Kawamura conceives of six typologies that "organize random thoughts and perspectives objectively":[72] (1) biological racism and stereotype reinforcement; (2) racial fetishism; (3) reinforcement of historical oppressions; (4) religious and spiritual blasphemy; (5) misuse of indigenous cultural traditions, textile motifs, and artisanal techniques; (6) exploitation of the economically challenged: class privilege.[73]

The typologies are expansive. Highlighting social constructs that are mutable and emotionally charged, Kawamura demonstrates why analysis of the causes and consequences of cultural appropriation within fashion is hard to discern. She also enlarges the scope of cultural appropriation, which becomes something of an umbrella term, to include the reinforcement of stereotypes, cultural insensitivities, and blasphemy.[74] These infractions may derive from the same ignorance and disrespect that causes cultural appropriation, and they may lead to cultural appropriation. Nonetheless, to cause offense and to show disrespect does not mean that something is being appropriated—taken—without permission and acknowledgment. To some extent, the entangling of transgressions that Kawamura presents through her typologies reflect present-day realities. Since the inception of social media "countless ideas [have been] unapologetically taken from other cultures" because "boundaries are not set, and the rules are almost non-existent in the virtual space."[75] To conflate cultural appropriation with an ignorant and indiscriminate cultural pilfering that is characteristic of a digitized global society emphasizes de-materiality, equivalence, and ambivalence, which have become hallmarks of "western" modernity. Kawamura suggests that questions of authenticity, the creation and defense of physical and figurative boundaries, which cultural appropriation debates typically dwell upon, become "futile" in the "globalized world."[76] Nonetheless, in appearing to accept "deterritorialization," "which supposedly makes the world flat, democratic, and egalitarian," she prioritizes a "western" outlook.[77] This lessens the dynamic of authority and control within acts of cultural appropriation and potentially marginalizes the indignation and emotional hurt that it causes.

The wide-ranging scope of Kawamura's typologies highlight one of the main challenges of approaching the subject of cultural appropriation. The term itself is anglophone. The concept of possession has a specific and forceful resonance within the "west."

Even when the focus of discussion shifts from the solely material and from questions of authenticity and ownership, which can perpetuate binary arguments between "you versus me" or "insider versus outsider," deterritorialization still prioritizes a "western" perspective because it is framed by the concept of modernity.[78] A "western" emphasis will always exist to some degree within discussions of appropriation and cultural appropriation because of the origins of the terms, as explained above. Nonetheless, their usage can be purposeful, as the suggestions of Pham, de Jong, and Kawamura establish, provided this cultural weight and the distortion that comes with it is fully acknowledged. Another approach is to be overtly pragmatic and focus on the degree to which appropriation occurs or the process by which it happens. The Cultural Authentication Process conceived by Toyne Erekosima and Joanna Eicher is one example.

The Cultural Authentication Process could be said to complement Karamura's typologies in so far as it emphasizes "that nothing is pure or authentic in this world."[79] Nonetheless, it is substantially different because it views appropriation as largely positive. They argue that appropriation creates a "genuine learning situation" between and within cultures.[80] In time, items of clothing become "a vital, valued part of the adopting culture's dress."[81] Erekosima and Eicher do not reference Homi K. Bhabha's concept of hybridity, but the "adaptive equilibrium" that results through their theory appears analogous to the "cultural contemporaneity" and "human, historic commonality" that he suggests occurs when different cultures positively acknowledge and purposefully adapt from one another.[82]

The theory of cultural appropriation responds to Erekosima's and Eicher's study of the dress of the Kalabari men of Nigeria. The dress of Kalabari people is deeply meaningful. Different colors, materials, cuts, and length of cloth convey specific messages about a person's social role and status. It is also characterized by the incorporation and adaptation of clothing elements from different communities and cultures.[83] The dress of Kalabari men changed markedly from the sixteenth century in response to European incursions into Africa.[84]

How Kalabari men incorporated European styles into their dress and ascribed new meanings and names to them is clarified through the cultural authentication process, which consists of four progressive stages: (1) selection, (2) characterization, (3) incorporation, and (4) transformation.

The stages do not have any strict duration and boundaries between them can blur. In the first stage, representatives of a culture will collectively select an item of dress from another culture to be included into theirs. The motivation and timing of this selection will vary for different artifacts, but choices are typically based on an object's perceived ability to improve lives, psychologically or physically. In the second stage, the chosen object will be reconceived, typically with a new name from the adopting culture's language that aligns with the function and purpose they want it to serve. Renaming the object establishes it within its new community and culture. In the third stage, effective incorporation of the object is demonstrated through its increasingly defined role within the social structures of its adopted culture and widespread usage among relevant individuals and groups. During the fourth stage the object undergoes further adaptations in response to its continued usage over a prolonged period. Through these changes it becomes fully incorporated and is no longer perceived as borrowed.[85]

The discontinuous application of Erekosima and Eicher's Cultural Authentication theory may be a consequence of the Eurocentric focus of much anglophone clothing-based research. There are still few studies that dwell on the relationships between "western" and non-"western" forms of dress. Nonetheless, there are clear strengths with Erekosima's and Eicher's study. First, cultural appropriation is established as a complex, even diffuse, phenomenon that involves many people, sometimes over many years. Curator and Asian scholar John Vollmer suggests that "cultural assimilation and transformation is global and has undoubtedly existed for millennia."[86] He also asserts that cultural authentication "nearly always entails a host of tangible and intangible conditions on the part of the receiving culture. These may include issues of religion, social order, gender, or culture, as well as psychological and even philosophical attitudes," but concedes that its documentation is fragmentary. Second, the theory moves us away from the analytical cul-de-sac caused by a focus on binaries—"right–wrong," "victim–victor," etc. Third, the authors avoid a strict focus on possession. As Kawamura observes, they demonstrate that "cultural products and artifacts are almost always influenced by external cultures."[87] This premise is the foundation of communication studies scholar Richard Rogers' model for understanding appropriation, which emphasizes the importance of transculturation.

In contrast to the scholars mentioned so far, Richard Rogers' engagement with appropriation does not start with an act of theft or adaptation. It is also important to note that Rogers does not directly consider fashion, although his ideas and conclusions are applicable to the industry and the ideas presented above. His point of departure is what he perceives to be the lack of clarity within academic debates about what qualifies as appropriation.[88] Conceiving of a model to analyze cultural exchange, Rogers seeks to provide clarity to discussions that are often characterized by their lack of definition and undertheorization.[89] His aim is not dissimilar to Pham's, although it is more dispassionate because he asserts that "cultural appropriation is inescapable when cultures come into contact, including virtual or representational contact."[90] Moreover, he frames his analysis with academic discussions of appropriation, rather than specific instances of it, making his intellectual contribution more of a critique of existing methodologies and their underlying assumptions.

Rogers identifies four types of appropriation within academic literature: cultural exchange; cultural dominance; cultural exploitation or cultural resistance; transculturation.[91] From these, he defines five terms: (1) Cultural exchange; (2) Cultural dominance; (3) Cultural resistance; (4) Cultural exploitation; (5) Transculturation. Briefly explained, these terms are conceived to provide greater clarity by envisaging appropriation as a nuanced phenomenon where binary notions of "good," "bad," "victim," "perpetrator" have little validity. Cultural exchange describes the "reciprocal exchange of symbols, artifacts, genres, rituals, or technologies between cultures with symmetrical power."[92] Within academic studies this equal and mutually respectful form of exchange is rarely discussed. It is typically invoked as an ideal to define "ethical standards by which other types of appropriation should be judged."[93] Rogers acknowledges the challenge of identifying "pure" forms of cultural exchange because relationships of power between individuals, groups, and cultures are seldom equal.[94] Querying the realization of this form of appropriation, he defines cultural dominance, his second category, as the "unidirectional imposition of elements of a dominant culture onto a subordinated (marginalized, colonized) culture."[95] Even accepting an unequal power relationship, the extent to which one culture will influence another varies. Rogers refers to "strategies of assimilation" where the imposition of a dominant culture is negotiated by the subordinate power. He identifies various tactics—assimilation, integration, intransigence, mimicry, resistance—that elucidate the contingency and often protracted nature of these negotiations.[96] The Cultural Authentication Process is not cited by Rogers, but it would be an example of integration because of the "internalization of some [of] the imposed culture without (complete) displacement or erasure of native culture and identity."[97] As an aside, it is interesting to reflect that academic discussions of appropriation, within fashion and beyond, generally do not build upon existing scholarship. In part, this reflects the disparate nature of scholarly engagement with the subject and its focus within certain disciplines—chiefly, film, literature, and music—and, within fashion, specifically, the discontinuous nature of its theorization.

Cultural resistance, Rogers' third category, acknowledges that the dominance of a superordinate culture is never likely total. He refers to the "agency and inventiveness" of subordinate cultures, which is rarely fully curtailed. Following philosopher Judith Butler and drawing upon a line of argument within critical and cultural studies that maintains there are multiple meanings and messages within media texts, Rogers asserts that "the very discourses that perpetuate the marginalization of subordinate groups can provide a basis for agency and resistance via appropriation and resignification."[98] In essence, although cultural exploitation envisages a scenario where one culture might take from another culture with impunity, it is too simplistic to conceive of exploitation along a binary, which debates about cultural appropriation tend to perpetuate.[99] Cultural exploitation, the fourth category, is most like cultural appropriation because a dominant culture treats a subordinate culture as a "mine" to be quarried in support of its own interests.[100] This type of appropriation is framed by four concerns highlighted by Ziff and Rao in their writing on cultural appropriation, which find parallels in Pham's conception of racial plagiarism; namely, that cultural appropriation contributes to cultural degradation, material deprivation for the people whose culture is being plundered, and a diminished acknowledgment of people's sovereign claims. Moreover, appropriative acts are never appreciative, and they do not constitute a form of cultural preservation.[101]

The final type of appropriation defined by Rogers is transculturation. This refers to an "ongoing" and "circular" process that involves the creation of cultural elements "through appropriations from and by multiple cultures such that identification of a single originating culture is problematic."[102] The cultural elements produced through transculturation are hybrid, although Rogers does not refer to Bhabha. Bhabha's work is nonetheless important for understanding the implications of what Rogers says about this form of appropriation because it "engages multiple lines of difference simultaneously."[103] Unlike the three previous types of appropriation that he defines, which prioritize a relationship between a superordinate and subordinate culture, transculturation conceives of multiple cultures, each with different levels of coercive power, continually intermingling and influencing one another. Consequently, this form of appropriation challenges a central premise of "western" thought that cultures exist as distinct, monolithic forms.[104] This form of appropriation aligns with

Kawamura's and de Jong's assertion that nothing is "authentic." Rogers observes that while "purity, wholeness, and integrity" might be perceived within and about some cultures, this is really no more than a reassuring and self-justifying "western" fiction. The more complicated, potentially sobering, certainly realistic situation is "that appropriations do not simply occur between cultures, constituting their relationships, but that such appropriative relations and intersections constitute the cultures themselves."[105]

The promise of transculturation is not without peril. Academics and cultural commentators might claim to pursue accuracy and clarity, but the stories humans tell themselves, framed by the socialized values and behaviors of their respective cultures, are so compelling that they frequently, if inadvertently, hinder the process of analysis.

Rogers suggests that the challenge transculturation poses to "western" ideas may mean that critics retain existing categories of appropriation, "at least until the political affiliations of transculturation are further clarified."[106]

Reflections

The ability to engage accurately, deeply, and sensitively with cases of appropriation in fashion is stymied by the anglophone words and socialized ideas they reinforce. Scholars have suggested new phrases and concepts to overcome this investigative stranglehold—including inappropriate discourse, racial plagiarism, transculturation—but these endeavors emphasize how far an academic discourse about appropriation is largely divorced, through time and place, from that which occurs between consumers, brands, and journalists. A review of different analyses of appropriation highlights three points of commonality that suggest the advantage gained through the creation of new intellectual models and terms is more apparent than actual. The points of commonality, which the above authors suggest should inform studies of appropriation in fashion, are as follows:

- **Dispassionate**. Studies of appropriation in fashion ought to prioritize facts over feelings. Objective details about the appropriative act should frame analysis rather than people's perceptions, which are contingent and consequently fallible.
- **Inclusive**. Analysis of appropriative acts should include consideration of all parties effected, rather than an overreliance on the views of "western" designers.
- **Nuanced**. A thorough analysis of appropriation in fashion requires analysts to be aware of the cultural and social circumstances that frame the appropriative act. In particular, there should be an awareness of how historical factors influence behaviors and attitudes in the present.

2
WHERE ARE WE NOW?

Reports of the hurt caused by appropriation within the fashion industry are commonplace in the "western" anglophone media. Stories in newspapers, blogs, and online forums, which can include expert testimonies, passionate interviews, and statistics that appear to confirm the worst preconceptions about the industry's inequalities, typically respond to the perceived infractions of a designer or brand after discussions have trended on social media. Amplified by the comments and expressive emoticons of people from around the world, the initial post often originates with a disenfranchised consumer, occasionally a concerned insider. The misgivings of one person become viral because they enflame a tension felt by many more. The sequence sketched here is generalized, but it is important to reflect that most of the reported cases of appropriation within fashion start with consumers. Much of the discussion about a perceived transgression is conducted openly, across freely accessible online platforms (albeit platforms that are more accessible within the "west"). Representatives of the fashion industry become involved when they are presented with a case to answer in the court of public opinion, as defendants. Academics are rarely involved until the case has been heard, and at this stage their role is often to contextualize and make sense of what has occurred. One implication of this simplified narrative is that the sustained explanation and theorization of the offenses caused by appropriation, which involves scholars, often occurs without the direct engagement of public opinion. Academic discourses about appropriation certainly happen through less publicly accessible channels of communication, most commonly conferences and journal articles. Consequently, many of the models and viewpoints summarized in the previous chapter are probably unknown to most of the people who are more likely to initiate and interrogate cases of appropriation within the fashion industry.

Cultural scholar Minh-Ha T. Pham has expressed frustration with the current form of cultural appropriation debates involving the fashion industry. For her, these discussions are a circular "performance" in which "nobody seems to change opinions for the next go-round."[1] Nonetheless, in her acknowledgment that "almost all matters of fashion ethics are now discussed, negotiated, and carried out online," she contends that social media consumers can place a significant amount of pressure on fashion businesses through their "quick-fire communications."[2] A focus of her argument is that the proliferation of online regulatory action inadvertently galvanizes "western" ethics and values, making the democratization of social media more apparent than actual. Immediately relevant to a consideration of the form of debates about appropriation is the realization that there are many discussions, involving different groups of people with different motivations, occurring simultaneously. At the very least, the academics devising the theories reviewed in the previous chapter do not, for the most part, have the same intentions as consumers communicating through social media. While reductionist, it is generally the case that the latter seek to apportion blame and derive recompense; the former analyze the extent to which either is appropriate, ethically and materially.

The plurality of the discussions about appropriation in fashion and the fact they frequently occur in siloed echo chambers is not deleterious, although it can contribute to a sense that conversations recur without resolution. The different people, stages, and arenas involved in discussions will also inform their content, outcomes, and impact. This can mean that some conversations become more passionate or more publicized without necessarily making an objectively purposeful contribution to the phenomenon. These points are important to keep in mind when reflecting on the cases of appropriation discussed in this chapter. In all, six episodes of appropriation and cultural appropriation are considered. While the selection inevitably reflects my preoccupations as a scholar and consumer, I have tried, first, to ensure that each considers a different aspect of the phenomenon of appropriation in fashion to demonstrate its complexity and prevalence. Second, I have tried to identify cases that highlight something fundamental about appropriation and its conception, rather than go down the "most notorious" route. Instances of appropriation and cultural appropriation within fashion are legion and many more will be reported and negotiated during the period that I work on this book. My intention has therefore been to select episodes that will be insightful in the immediate and longer term, and which include a range of examples, from a specific garment to a whole campaign, a type of dress associated with a specific community, to a legal tussle between two fashion heavyweights. The episodes considered are: a sweater from Gucci's autumn/winter 2018 collection "Cyborg; Dior's 2019 ready-to-wear cruise collection; a garment from Rwanda-based Moshions' spring/summer 2018 collection; queer fashion; The Proud Boy's adoption of a Fred Perry polo shirt in 2020; and a copyright infringement case brought by Adidas AG against Thom Browne Inc. in 2021.

As a final introductory note, language, considered in Chapter 1, is a key part of my analysis. After all, how we come to know about a case of appropriation and perceive what is at stake because of it, is typically through somebody else's words, whether this be a tweet, a newspaper report, or an academic essay.

In particular, I argue that the language used by anglophone fashion journalists reporting on fashion collections evidences and embeds "western" socialized values that make appropriation more likely because it presents the phenomenon as commonplace. A consideration of language used by contemporary fashion commentators and news reporters is important when thinking through appropriation and cultural appropriation because "fashion journalism reflects all of fashion's polarities and contradictions," in the words of fashion scholars Rosie Findlay and Johannes Reponen.[3] In making this claim, they follow social and cultural studies scholar Agnès Rocamora, who argues that "the fabrication of fashion becomes not just the fabrication of the material object known as the fashion dress but the fabrication of ideas about fashion, the creation of beliefs that give it meaning, whether it be as popular culture . . . or as high culture."[4] In what follows, I seek to develop earlier observations about the causes of appropriation by arguing that the language used to negotiate the phenomenon of appropriation and cultural appropriation is a significant, and overlooked, contributory factor to its continued occurrence.

Episode 1. Gucci, "Cyborg," Autumn/ Winter, Menswear and Womenswear, 2018

I start with a widely reported case of appropriation in fashion that could probably be deemed typical in terms of the cause of the offense—in this case, a single garment—the public commentary, and media reporting around it, and the response from the fashion brand involved. However, there remain details about the episode that have not previously been acknowledged in the ensuing scholarship despite it being subject to in-depth analysis.[5] In February 2019, a sweater from Gucci's autumn/winter 2018 collection "Cyborg" was widely criticized within the anglophone media for being culturally appropriated and racist. The distinctive design of the garment, which featured an oversize neck that covered the lower third of the wearer's face and an oval aperture framed by red wool for the mouth, was likened to blackface.[6] Several garments in the collection had a similar appearance. English scholar Ayanna Thompson defines blackface as "the application of any prosthetic—makeup, soot, burnt cork, minerals, masks, etc.—to imitate the complexion of another race."[7]

In response to negative comments on X (then, Twitter), which appear to have been the source of this grievance, Gucci apologized for

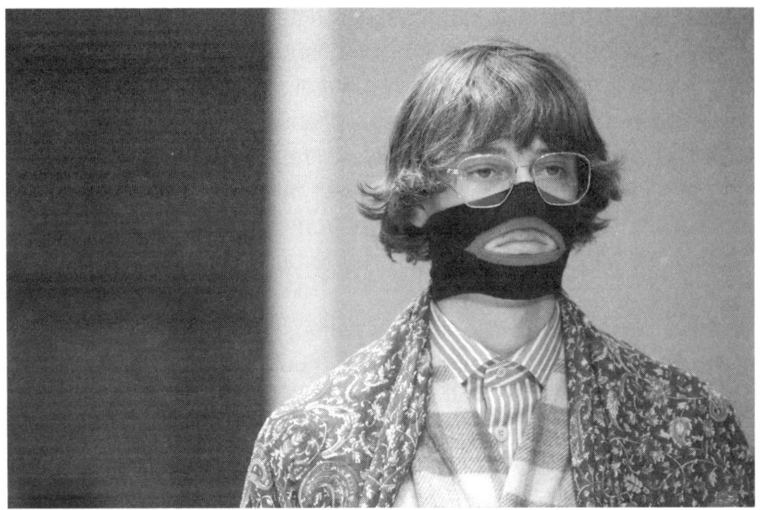

IMAGE 6 Detail from Gucci's 'Cyborg' collection, 2018.
Source: Getty images.

the offense caused via its X account and withdrew the $890 sweater from sale. Harlem-based African-American designer Daniel Day, or Dapper Dan as he is more commonly known within the industry, condemned Gucci through a post on his Instagram account. He said the brand had "gotten it outrageously wrong."[8] Asserting that he was "a Black man before … a brand," he seemed to imply that his creative partnership with Gucci was in jeopardy.[9] To assuage the designer's misgivings, as much to respond to public qualms in a debate that was gaining traction across social media, Gucci president and CEO Marco Bizzarri traveled from Italy to the United States. Following a meeting with Dan, community members, and fashion industry representatives, Gucci announced that it would initiate a four-point action plan that included "hiring global and regional directors for diversity and inclusion, setting up a multicultural design scholarship program, launching a diversity and inclusivity awareness program [and] launching a global exchange program."[10] Bizzarri and Gucci creative director

Alessandro Michele also issued statements to the press.[11] Bizzarri's tone was aloof. He asserted that the offending garment was caused by "cultural ignorance."[12] While his intention is unknowable, such a sweeping remark made the brand's offense at once too large and too opaque to critique effectively. By contrast, Michele was defensive. He claimed the attribution of racism was misplaced. The meaning of the sweater was "completely different from what was ascribed [to it]" because he had intended the garment to be a tribute to performance artist and designer Leigh Bowery.[13] Briefly sketched, the preceding narrative played out over a ten-day period, between the appearance of the first critical comments on social media on February 6 and the announcement of Gucci's plan on February 15.

On the face of it, the case bears out Pham's observation that social media pressure can be as quick as it is decisive in prompting companies to reappraise their actions in response to public qualms. It also appears to give credence to her view that discussions about cultural appropriation in fashion tend to take a predictable format. The people involved, the statements made, and the initial outcomes agreed to quell the emotional intensity sparked by Gucci's sweater, seem noteworthy only for being like other episodes of cultural appropriation, prior and subsequent to this incident. The sense of parallelism is largely a consequence of fashion journalists, whose analysis of fractious industry incidents tends to proceed by comparison. For example, when Burberry's autumn/winter 2020 ready-to-wear collection Tempest was criticized for appearing to glorify suicide, several journalists made comparisons to Gucci's sweater, which had dominated headlines during the preceding week. Save for the fact that these were two large luxury fashion brands causing offense, the events were not at all similar.[14] Bland analysis like this retards criticism and reduces the likelihood of meaningful lessons being learned from the incidents. Bizzarri's and Michele's comments are notable because they suggest the men were more concerned to end discussion about the sweater than they were willing to reflect on its causes and consequences. This was chiefly because neither one appeared to think there was a substantial case to answer. Bizzarri's suggestion that his brand did not know the hurt it had caused, and Michele's assertion that the fault was misattributed because his designs had not been interpreted as he intended, are examples of white innocence. Coined by Thompson in her study of blackface, the term is useful, if slightly expanded, to describe racist actions committed by white people whose depiction of black people is, first, ignorant of the hurt they can cause and, second, presumed permissible, perhaps even legitimate, because of the longstanding prevalence of white people depicting black people within "western" culture.[15]

Nonetheless, there is a layer of complexity regarding these public exchanges that consumers, brand representatives, commentators, and, later, scholars did not consider. In 2019, public discussion about the sweater became politically charged at the time of the collection's retail launch, which coincided with Black History Month in the United States.[16] At the same time, journalist Amy Held, writing for the American media organization NPR, drew attention to several race-related news stories that were making headlines across the country involving several politicians—she focuses on Virginia's Governor Ralph Northam and Attorney General Mark Herring—who had worn blackface during their college years.[17] However, when the collection debuted in a different country almost a year earlier in February 2018 no concerns were raised about race and the few comments that were made about cultural appropriation did not gain traction.[18] This included criticisms from the U.S. Sikh community, who expressed concern that the turban, which appeared in several of the show's looks, was a "sacred article of faith … not a mere fashion accessory."[19]

Journalists who reported on "Cyborg" during Milan Fashion Week in 2018 expressed a mixture of confusion and admiration for a collection that included one model holding a baby dragon and a white female wearing a Pagoda-style hat.[20] Fashion scholars Paul Jobling, Philippa Nesbitt, and Angelene Wong, who take a largely positive view of a "hugely playful" collection, note that "Cyborg's" plurality of visual messages even stymied a commentator with a doctorate.[21]

Nonetheless, while opinions diverged, there was consensus that the ninety looks, "unnerving" as they were, confirmed Michele's creative acumen.[22] Most reporters followed British journalist Sarah Mower who remarked on the "zillion billion clothes and accessories guaranteed to stoke Instagram commentaries for weeks to come."[23] To my knowledge, journalist Tahmina Begum, writing for *The Huffington Post*, was the only commentator to identify some concerns, relayed through social media, that Michele's designs constituted cultural appropriation, but her report does not mention blackface.[24] Writing in 2022, Jobling, Nesbitt, and Wong make reference to a "knitted blackface mask" and "golliwog blackface woollen masks."[25] They also cite Pham's concept of racial plagiarism. The trio acknowledge that some of Michele's designs usurped the creative, cultural, and economic control of their source communities, but their analysis focuses on how the racial inequalities within "Cyborg" emphasized a broader trait within Michele's collections and catwalk presentations, whereby his ambitious ideas flounder because of their inherent ambiguity.[26] Without referencing it, the authors appear to accept Richard Rogers' concept of transculturation, which contends that appropriative acts are not marginal but mainstream and constitute culture itself.[27] Consequently, they consider the collection's sweaters and balaclavas to be no more than a form of "terrorist chic."[28] The inclination to consider the collection's head- and face-concealing garments benign follows Mower, who suggested the balaclavas referenced "a postoperative state" when writing about the collection in 2018.[29]

The fact that a public, at times acrimonious, discussion about cultural appropriation and racism within "Cyborg" occurred in 2019 nearly twelve months after the collection was first shown in 2018 demonstrates a troubling ambivalence about these phenomena within fashion design, specifically, and fashion consumption, in which I include journalism, broadly. The public outcry sparked by Gucci's sweater in 2019 was contingent upon the product's retail launch occurring during Black History Month within the United States against a backdrop of news stories relaying historic race-related offensives committed by serving American politicians.

IMAGE 7 The Gucci runway for 'Cyborg', shown during Milan Fashion Week, 2018.
Source: Getty images.

While the intensity of the ensuing discussions and Gucci's actions indicate the depth of hurt caused by appropriation when it reproduces offensive stereotypes, at least two counterfactual questions can be asked. First, if the product launch for Cyborg had occurred during a different month and news cycle and within a different country, would accusations of cultural appropriation and racism have been raised? Second, would these concerns have been sustained to the same degree? These questions are thought experiments, but they demonstrate the precarity of the concept of cultural appropriation. Consequently, it is difficult to apply the scholarly analyses discussed in the previous chapter to this episode, which in effect constitutes two experiences of cultural appropriation: one, which occurred in 2018 and went largely unnoticed, and a second, in 2019, which inflamed popular opinion when it was linked to contemporary circumstances that highlighted the persistence of systemic racism. This episode emphasizes the prevalence of racial inequality and white innocence within the fashion industry, which effectively hid Gucci's infraction for twelve months behind a veil of ignorance.

Episode 2. Dior Womenswear Cruise Ready-to-Wear, Spring/Summer 2019

The second episode develops points from the first in its focus on another luxury "western" fashion brand, Dior. Within a six-month period, a widely praised example of cultural appreciation by the brand's former creative director Maria Grazia Chiuri became an example of cultural appropriation. My analysis reflects on the contemporary reception and reporting of this collection and thinks critically about who is speaking. How? When? To whom? Responses to these questions emphasize the importance of contingency in discussions of appropriation. They show how a change in circumstance is fundamental in the determination of whether a designer's or brand's actions come to be labeled as appropriation. The discussion bears out Pham's observation that the criminalization of a copyist is determined "by social and economic power," which tends to favor white "western" people.[30]

Dior's ready-to-wear cruise collection for 2019 was inspired by Mexico's *escaramuza*, a term meaning "skirmish" that is more readily associated with female riders and their distinctive appearance, which includes flat wide-brimmed hats, high-waisted full skirts, and delicate bands of intricate embroidery. The eighty-two looks of the collection were widely praised within the "western" anglophone press when they debuted at the Château de Chantilly in May 2018. Journalist Jenni Avins, writing for online news platform Quartz, opined that "in an age where critics are wont to cry 'cultural appropriation,' Chiuri stepped carefully to pull off a respectful tribute, melding the traditions of Mexican dress with Dior's French heritage."[31] However, six months later, the "west's" anglophone press adopted a contrary stance. Scathing denunciations followed the announcement that Jennifer Lawrence, a white actor, would front the associated campaign. Citing posts from social media users, *The Daily Mail* newspaper reported on the perceived cultural sleight to Mexican women, who did not feature in the campaign, by claiming that Dior had been "SLAMMED."[32] Capitalization presumably highlighted the affront. The stark reappraisal of Dior's collection within a six-month period exposes an instability in the interpretation of cultural appropriation, which appears, paradoxically, to be as strongly felt as it is allusive to securely identify and define.

To have a white American woman front a campaign that had been inspired by Mexico's *escaramuza* was considered offensive.[33] Insult was added to injury when Lawrence spoke of her desire to celebrate

IMAGE 8 Jennifer Lawrence poses at a photo call during for Dior during Paris Fashion Week, 2020.
Source: Getty images.

"these women's heritage through such a modern lens."[34] The implication that people who were not Mexican were determining the contemporary relevance of an aspect of Mexican culture was derided by social media users, who found grist for their mill when Lawrence revealed that her photographic shoot was staged in California.[35] As reasonable as these concerns and criticisms seem, it is noteworthy that similar remarks were not made about the collection when it debuted six months previously.

While it was considered offensive to shoot the cruise campaign in the United States rather than Mexico, the decision to show the collection in France was generally welcomed, because Chantilly is "known for [its] delicate lace and sturdy equestrians."[36] Journalist Alexander Fury coined the punning term "PexMex" to describe the collection's "fusion" of traditions from Dior, France, and Mexico.[37] He asserts that the hybrid designs were not as strange as they may have seemed "because Chiuri discovered the distinct similarities to explore, and the differences to ignore" between Mexican and French traditions.[38] Fury does not elaborate on these details and is content that Chiuri alone identified what was appropriate to accept and reject. A tendency to declare without demonstration is apparent in other reports of the collection. Journalist Dominique Muret's account for online news site FashionNetwork alludes to cultural appropriation in her observation that "Chiuri managed to avoid the temptation of indulging in exotic folklore, employing references to these Mexican amazons with respect and finesse," but does not fully engage with the topic.[39] She cites the "bright colors of the embroideries" and "braiding which decorated the long cotton dresses, black on white or vice versa," but does not explain how far these design elements were adapted from their Mexican exemplars.[40]

Performance of the equestrian event, the *charreria*, has become conspicuous as an expression of Mexican identity during the twentieth century and forms part of the annual independence celebrations, but there is a longer history to this cultural activity that includes the dress of *adelitas*, groups of women who fought during Mexico's revolutionary war between 1910 and 1920. Both the presentation and reporting of Dior's collection tends to denude the *escaramuza* dress of its historical meaning and utility, reducing it to a series of shapes and patterns that can be freely re-contextualized.[41] Moreover, while it is probably inadvertent colloquialism, to write of "temptation" and indulgence implies that Muret considers cultural appropriation to be commonplace within the fashion industry and that Chiuri's collection is atypical for not following an established pattern of behavior.

Fury's language, redolent as it is of the "west's" search and acquisition for resources during the eighteenth and nineteenth centuries, is equally revealing. He suggests Chiuri's discovery of the *escaramuza* was an especially "perfect find" because Dior had incorporated designs from Mexico in one of its early twentieth-century collections. The brand's Adelita style "was the new look of 1910–20, the years of the Mexican Revolutionary War."[42] Establishing a linkage between Dior's collections of the past and present, Fury's argument assumes the aesthetic utility of Mexican culture in the previous century justified its re-use in the present. To make this connection, he flattens chronologies. He does not acknowledge that cultural values have shifted during the intervening century and that the concept of cultural appropriation did not exist at the time of Dior's earlier collection. Distorting time and history, Fury can simultaneously observe that designs within Chiuri's collection possessed a distinctive Dior silhouette without considering the moral weight of his remark that Christian Dior, the brand's founder and namesake, regarded the "notion of the Amazon woman [as] something of an anathema."[43]

There are several problems with the term "Amazon," which can be traced to ancient Greece where it referred to a formidable and independent female warrior. It has been used to serve many causes in the "west," variously to chide and champion the social and political rights of women. Christian Dior's usage appears particularly pejorative and reflects gendered hierarchies that were more prevalent during the twentieth century. If a geographical reference was, in fact, intended by using the term "Amazon," Dior's remark was also wide of the mark because the Amazon River and region is over 5,000 kilometers south of Mexico. Elaboration is not provided because this becomes another detail that is smoothed over for Fury—and for Muret, who wrote of "Mexican amazons"—to make his argument that Chiuri's collection was about "strident, strong femininity—motivated, militant, and free."[44] Compelling as these ideas are, Fury's chronological discontinuity and moral obliviousness seem to prevent him from observing that these are ideas that resonate most readily within a post-millennial "western" frame.

The presentation of the cruise collection in Chantilly was equally celebrated within the "western" press in May, and similarly characterized by explanatory rifts. Muret's report is rhapsodic about the "unforgettable experience" that Chiuri arranged.[45] Her description of eight *escaramuza*, who were apparently flown from Mexico to open the event, is interesting for its unselfconscious bias. The riders waited outside the covered runway and were "soaked to the skin" because of a passing storm.[46] "They were afforded some protection by large sombreros."[47] Their participation in the catwalk presentation is passed over with the remark that "the end of this equestrian demonstration signaled the beginning of the runway show."[48] By contrast, the models who followed the *escaramuza*, a majority (82 percent) of whom were white, were described as "braving the driving rain and the treacherous catwalk."[49] "Thankfully," they had suitable footwear and were "protected" by hats created by "famous milliner Stephen Jones."[50] While these words, phrases, and subject matter do not relate directly to the topic of cultural appropriation, the unequal response to the *escaramuza* and models they establish facilitates the construction of a value system where it could occur. Here, there is an implicit parallel with sociologist Yuniya Karamura's typologies, reviewed in the previous chapter, which emphasize how fashion designs can enact and perpetuate cultural stereotypes.[51]

The *escaramuza* inspired Dior's collection but their cultural significance within Mexico is not deeply explored in any of the anglophone commentaries. In explaining the women's role in the *charreada*, Muret proceeds to negate their unique appearance in "traditional Mexican petticoat dresses" by suggesting how effortlessly Chiuri merged these garments with "the savoir-faire of Dior's ateliers and its unique Parisian touch."[52] A fuller account of the *escaramuza* and their cultural heritage is provided by Fury in the first paragraph of his article, but his decision to commence the second paragraph with the justificatory remark, "Long preamble," hints at a belief that readers would not consider this information interesting or relevant.[53]

The clothing and staging of Dior's cruise collection in May 2018 had sufficient incongruities to raise queries about cultural appropriation, but none, to my knowledge, were voiced by the reporting press. I contend that this was because the content and choreography of the Chantilly show conformed to expectations of how a catwalk presentation by a luxury fashion brand should appear within the "west." Only when some of these incongruities were highlighted by their appearance

IMAGE 9 The escaramuza during an Independence Day Parade in Mexico, 2023.
Source: Getty images.

on the body of a non-Mexican woman (Jennifer Lawrence), who appeared in still images far removed from fashion insiders and the captivating atmosphere created within France, were concerns raised by consumers, many of whom were likely seeing the collection for the first time.

While the collection by Maria Grazia Chiuri for Dior in 2019 is very different to that by Alessandro Michele for Gucci in 2018, parallels exist between the reception and reporting of the appropriative acts within them. First, in both cases initial comments by fashion reporters tended to be positive. They turned negative only after concerns were raised by consumers about appropriation on social media. This fact raises questions about the role of fashion journalism within the industry and the voices it prioritizes, which are rarely considered within discussions of appropriation. Second, the cases prompt a broader consideration of what constitutes fashion. They certainly provide a reminder that fashion, following Karamura, exists as a belief in people's minds.[54] The cases suggest that commentators and insiders consider appropriation an axiom of fashion design. Consequently, they can be tolerant of it, even oblivious to it. This is a key finding within fashion scholar Jennifer Ayre's study of appropriation within vintage designs.[55] Consumers, on the other hand, seem more critical of the phenomenon. These contrasting opinions suggest that multiple perceptions of appropriation circulate concurrently among different groups of people who have opposing views about its acceptability.

Communication studies scholar Richard Rogers encourages us to think about transculturation and the idea that appropriation exists as an "ongoing" and "circular" process. The example of Dior—and Gucci—suggest it could be helpful to conceptualize people's responses to appropriation in a similar way and to recognize that multiple and overlapping discussions occur together. This may lead to a more accurate understanding of how ideas of appropriation are contingent and shift across the fashion industry.

Episode 3. Moshions, "Intsinzi," Spring/ Summer 2018

People's perception of appropriation and the application of academic theories to explain specific cases of the phenomenon is clearly very complicated. The frustration that Pham has felt, the concerned outlook that Kawamura and de Jong express, seem reasonable, and relatable. The next episode provides further complications—and hopefully through these, some elucidation—by pursuing the concepts of cultural authentication and transculturation, articulated by Toyne Erekosima and Joanne Eicher, and Richard Rogers, respectively. I focus on a garment within the spring/summer 2018 "Intsinzi" (Victory) collection of Moshions, a fashion brand created by Rwandan designer Moïse (Moses) Turahirwa in 2015. The garment forms part of the permanent collection of the Victoria and Albert Museum, London, and was included within their *Africa Fashion* exhibition that ran between July 2022 and April 2023 at their South Kensington site. The ensemble consists of a tunic top and pair of trousers made from a blue-gray wool and viscose blend cloth.[56] Based on the *umushanana*, a long draped skirt associated with Rwandan royalty and females, the tunic is made of two parts that derive from the *umukenyero*, a wrapper, and *umwitero*, a draped sash. The torso covering is full-sleeved and mid-thigh length. It has a crew neck and single pleat buttoned cuffs. Across the front of the tunic, seven vertical pleats descend from the middle of the neckline to the hem. A detachable swag, a length of cloth identical to the tunic and trousers, is threaded under a band of fabric across the top of the tunic's left shoulder. It hangs in five folds across its front. On the right shoulder the swag is secured with press studs that are fixed to a band decorated with black and white glass beads in a geometric design. Over the back of the left shoulder the swag hangs straight, terminating at the tunic's hemline. The trousers appear slim cut. They have cuffs and a centrally ironed crease.

The Victoria and Albert Museum's online catalog describes Turahirwa's outfit as a "trouser suit." The top is referred to as a "shirt." Curators have adopted this anglophone shorthand despite acknowledging that the ensemble is based on the *umushanana* in the same catalog entry. Their anglicizing is possibly attributable to Turahirwa, who says he deliberately seeks to "reconstruct the traditional *umushanana* [with] contemporary new silhouettes."[57] The silhouette of his outfit does resemble a men's shirt and trousers, which is a familiar sight throughout the "west" and much of the world that has adopted its social structures. While the designer established Moshions "to explore Rwanda's fashion potential and embolden culture," he has implied that he avoids too close a focus on traditional Rwandan, or African, styles.[58] In his early collections, Turahirwa said he "stayed away from the *igitenge* (African fabric); I wanted my outfits [to be] unique; everyone else was using *igitenge*."[59] References to "new silhouettes," uniqueness, and "a modern touch" lack specificity, but it is clear that Turahirwa embraces "western" designs through his creation of bomber jackets, blazers, and cardigans.[60]

The African styles Turahirwa adapts may also have "western" influence. The draped sash that distinguished his contribution to the *Africa Fashion* exhibition is based on the *umwitero*, a garment that has been associated with Rwandan royalty since the 1920s. The origins of this sartorial adoption are unclear but as it occurred when Rwanda was controlled by Belgium—it replaced Germany after the First World War—it is possible they are traceable to the aiguillettes worn by senior army and navy officers in Europe, to which there is more than a passing resemblance.[61] While I have found no explicit evidence of a connection, scholar Michelle D. Wagner cites nineteenth-century German administrators and visitors who observed Rwandan royal dress, which they claim included "imported" clothing.[62] The source of the imports is not clarified, but examples exist from other African countries where royals incorporated European symbols into their clothing. For example, a beaded crown (*ade*) from the Yoruba of Nigeria, now in the collection of William D. and Norma Canelas Roth,

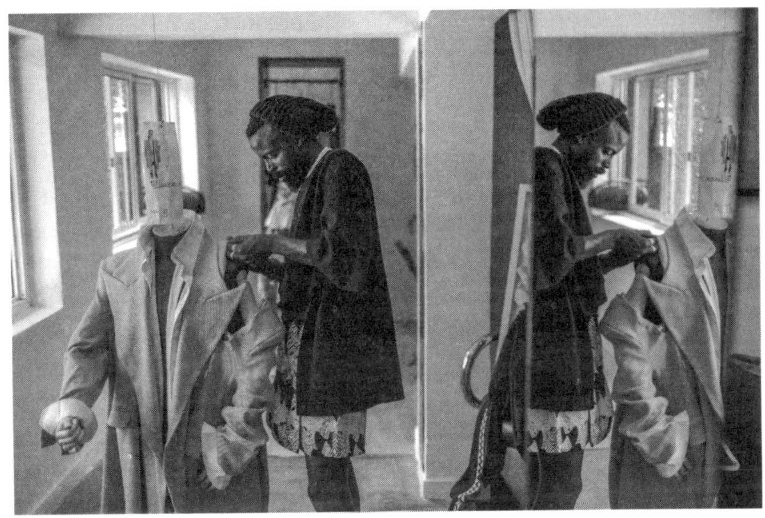

IMAGE 10 Designer Moses Turahirwa.
Source: Getty images.

imitates the shape of the British Imperial State Crown.[63] This act of mimicry was a response to the establishment of British rule in Nigeria during the nineteenth century. It would seem the Yoruba sought to buttress their traditions of royal authority by adapting a potent symbol of British rule and denuding it of its singular authority.

This crown is not unique. Variants across Africa include Christian iconography and crosses. In their conscious imitation of European styles, African crowns continued to incorporate regional symbols to augment the authority of their wearer. The *ade* from the Roth collection is decorated with four birds, "which represent the spiritual feminine power of older women that protects the crown."[64]

This discussion has necessarily moved us away from Turahirwa's designs. It suggests that in using the *umushanana* as the basis for his collections, he was adapting elements from his country's past that were in themselves adaptations. In the first instance, it may be possible to interpret the adoption of the *umwitero* by Rwanda's royalty during the 1920s in line with the Cultural Authentication Process.[65] As Erekosima and Eicher explain, an item of dress from another culture was selected and renamed to become part of Rwandan royal dress. Over time, the item was adapted, so much so that its place within the dress of Rwanda's rulers became accepted, normalized, to the point where its origins are not easily discernible, if they are sought at all. Consequently, Turahirwa can consider the object a bona fide part of his country's history of dress. The influence of the *umwitero* within his "Intsinzi" collection could also fit with the type of appropriation that Rogers terms transculturation.[66] This explains how cultural influences are multiple and continuous, such that it can be impossible, perhaps even unproductive, to locate a single source of inspiration. Implicit within transculturation is the negation of possession and cultural hierarchies. Rogers contends that cultural borrowing is infinite, such that "western" articulations that dwell on cultural exchanges within superordinate and subordinate relationships are too narrowly framed. His concept is also apt to explain the Victoria and Albert's anglicized interpretation of Turahirwa's designs, along with my own, as I seek to connect the *umwitero* to an item of dress more familiar to me through my cultural background, for two reasons. First, transculturation shows how the associations and connections that give meanings to objects are continually negotiated. They do not stop after the object has been conceived and created. Second, transculturation readily exposes a tendency, certainly within anglophone discourse, to assimilate objects within a "western" schema.

Episode 4. Queer Dress: Billy Porter and Harry Styles, 2021

Seeking to complicate and critically analyze the place of appropriation within fashion, this next episode moves the analysis away from a singular episode to consider appropriation that effects a community.

The intention is to elucidate how different perceptions of appropriation circulate concurrently. A focus on queer dress, which I define as the clothing and appearance of self-identified queer people that deliberately upends the "western" binaries of gender and sex, is contrived because members of these diverse communities do not dress alike. Moreover, in this analysis I am concentrating on atypical members—actors and celebrities—whose appearance can more conspicuously challenge "western" gender and sexual conventions. While the distinctions that I am making are somewhat artificial, they reflect public discussion about the ownership of a form of dress that is typically associated with people who identify as queer.

My starting point is an interview published within the UK's *The Sunday Times* in October 2021 with queer American actor and singer Billy Porter. In the article, Porter criticized fellow actor and singer British-born Harry Styles, whose membership of the queer community remains ambiguous, for his gender diverse dress.[67] Styles, who has been dressed by Gucci's former creative director Alessandro Michele and independent designer Harris Reed, has come to be known for wearing clothes and dress accessories that the "west" more conventionally associates within women, including dresses, skirts, pearl necklaces, and handbags. These style choices have prompted commentators to make comparisons between him and musicians David Bowie and Freddie Mercury.[68] This "gender-fluid fashion" has sparked discussion about Styles' sexuality and the extent to which he might be queer-baiting, seeking to appeal to members of the queer community without being a declared member of it.[69] Porter talked to these themes in his interview. He maintained that his decision to blur the male–female gender binary through his choice of public attire was "political." He claimed to have fought his whole life "to get to the place where I could wear a dress to the Oscars," which he did in 2018 and 2019.[70] In so doing, Porter believed he had "changed the whole game."[71] By contrast, he argued that all Harry Styles "has to do is be white and straight."[72] Porter's remarks came a month before the publication of the December 2021 issue of American *Vogue*, which featured Styles on the cover wearing a ballgown by Alessandro Michele. The image initiated a heated public debate about the extent to which this appearance was "revolutionary," a descriptor used by Michele.[73] In response to the cover shoot, Porter suggested Styles wore gender diverse clothing "because it's the thing to do."[74] Journalist Jireh Deng, writing for NPR, challenged Porter's stance for his suggestion that he "own[ed] a fashion genre . . . with a rich history led by countless other transgender and gay people of color."[75]

In this specific instance, Deng's position seems correct. Nobody can lay claim to a culturally, chronologically, and sartorially diverse form of appearance, which has been linked to various people irrespective of their gender identity and sexual preferences. Nonetheless, a similar case of what might be termed queer appropriation has been highlighted by poet and journalist Ariel Sobel. Here, the attribution of possession seems more equivocal. Sobel considers heterosexual people, chiefly actors and celebrities, who play queer people or temporarily adopt—appropriate—queer personas, as did singers Madonna and Britney Spears when they kissed at the MTV awards in 2003.[76] Sobel frames her discussion around transgender author Julia Serano's three constituents of appropriation—erasure, exploitation, denigration. She argues that the portrayal of queer people (bisexual specifically) in television and film amounts to an erasure because it is typically negative or dismissive on account of a character's bisexuality being depicted as a phase.[77] Portrayals are exploitative when a queer person is kissed by a heterosexual person. In this scenario they are turned into "an exotic sex move," which can be physically or psychologically damaging.[78] Portrayals denigrate queer people when elements of their culture, or queer people themselves, are used to entertain noncommunity members. The denigration can be especially damaging when it is undertaken by people in positions of privilege. Sobel places heterosexual people in this category, as did Porter when speaking about Styles.[79] Considered in the abstract and as a phenomenon that can encompass the arts sector broadly, Sobel's criticisms and concerns about queer appropriation by heterosexuals

IMAGE 11 David Bowie as Ziggy Stardust, 1972.
Source: Getty images.

appear to give weight to Porter's grievance against Styles; factually, because multiple examples can be cited to convey her misgivings, and morally, because the hurt she describes can be more readily

IMAGE 12 Billy Porter at the 91st Annual Academy Awards, 2019. Source: Getty images.

identified.[80] Nevertheless, Deng's query about whether a culture can be owned persists. These discussions underscore how concerns about the appropriation of queer culture through dress are largely framed by dominant gender and sexual binaries, which were defined in the "west" during the eighteenth and nineteenth centuries, along with an assumption, emerging during the same period, that culture can be possessed and restricted.[81]

The position taken by Porter and Sobel is also ahistorical. They do not consider that appropriation has long formed part of the public performance of queer identities within the "west." In her commentary on Porter, Deng cites a blog article about the history of voguing, a lavish and overtly performative form of dance that originated within Harlem's black and Latino queer communities. Voguing is highly appropriative and takes "from the poses in high fashion and ancient Egyptian art."[82] The wide popularity of *RuPaul's Drag Race* has also increased interrogation of the role of appropriation within drag among anglophone audiences on social media and through blogs.[83] Appropriative acts are typically considered to be an inherent part of these genres. For example, German photographer Parker Tilghman is emphatic that the satiric appropriation of cultural motifs is necessary to sustain drag's critique of social norms:

> Drag exists because of incorporating aspects of different cultures. Drag is a mimicking, a caricature, a mirror to the beauty and ridiculousness of society. Drag is an exaggeration and an examination and many times will be insulting, aggressive, and even wrong because at it's [*sic*] best drag should challenge people to think about their place in the fallacies of the world. Can that sometimes be racist? Yes, very much so because society is racist. Does it have the power to call out, combat, and correct that racism? Yes, very much so.[84]

The emphasis on incongruity and ridiculousness is important. Following philosopher Mikhail Bakhtin's examination of carnival laughter, it is now broadly recognized that collective humor has the potential to make established social concepts and structures seem risible and more easily resistible.[85] As I have argued elsewhere in relation to fancy dress costume, laughter can be considered a form of cultural jamming because it temporarily blocks people's critical antennae and permits the conveyance of less dominant viewpoints.[86] Consequently, the use of laughter can become a strategy of assimilation because the framing of a joke demonstrates an intimate, even insider, understanding of dominant cultural ideas. In this sense, appropriation becomes a tool that forcibly asserts social inclusion

IMAGE 13 Participants from Season Six of RuPaul's Drag Race UK. Source: Getty images.

through the demonstration of otherness. Public historian Tsione Wolde-Michael avers that voguers "seem to imitate the very structures that marginalize them."[87] Nonetheless, the situation is precarious as drag artist Portia B observes that black and white drag artists are treated unequally. She argues that white performers either wholly appropriate the look of black people or they utilize elements of black culture within their acts.[88] These concerns of racial inequality echo those of Porter, who suggested that Styles' whiteness facilitated his ability to utilize elements of dress more readily associated with womenswear within the "west."

What emerges through these discussions is a complicated picture of appropriation, which ostensibly occurs along two divides. One of these divides relates to a person's gender and sexual identity, as queer people and heterosexual people take elements of dress and appearance from each other. Another divide relates to race. Irrespective of gender or sexual identity, white people—Portia B suggests white men specifically—are considered more likely to engage in appropriative acts. However, regardless of position and intent, all disputants are engaged in some degree of appropriation. Consequently, what is at stake through these discussions is less what is being appropriated and how, than whose claim to appropriation is more justifiable.

This situation demonstrates how there can be myriad viewpoints about appropriation circulating concurrently. Moreover, within these discussions the appropriative act seems to be of secondary importance. The primary concern is to have the right to define what the act represents, and with this, the right to legitimize the act. This observation recalls Pham's assertion that the determination of guilt in cases of appropriation—and by the same token, verdicts of exoneration—are predicated on "social and economic power."[89] The observation also supports Rogers' contention that as much as appropriation is continuous, plural, inevitable, the dominance of "western" socialized thought means there is a tendency to approach the phenomenon through a binary that offers the seductive, distorting comfort that some cultures and people's rights possess greater validity.

A desire to establish security through cultural possession should not be underestimated. Political philosopher Frantz Fanon astutely recognized the comfort that people—typically white and of the "west"—felt for being able to shelter behind their national cultures.[90] Delice develops this point and asserts that the "emotional intensity" that typically characterizes people's response to (cultural) appropriation is the "manifestation of a wider disquiet in the face of the myriad forms of dispossession and labor exploitation perpetrated by the forces of today's egregiously unfair transnational capital accumulation, in addition to the material and psychological legacies of colonialism."[91] In this episode, the disquiet and security of possession looks to be framed by the marginalization experienced by members of the queer community in response to economic structures that compound colonialist mentalities.

Episode 5. Fred Perry and the Proud Boys

This fifth example develops the preceding discussion about ownership and entitlement. I consider how a single brand—Fred Perry—has responded flexibly, if inconsistently, to appropriative acts to variously popularize and protect its consumer appeal. This episode elucidates a recurrent theme of power by looking at the appropriative actions of a small, violent alt-right group that could ostensibly be described as subordinate when compared with the cultural and economic influence that make Fred Perry superordinate.

On September 24, 2020, Fred Perry issued a statement to explain that it had withdrawn its "Black/Yellow/Yellow twin tipped [polo] shirt" from sale within the United States and Canada. The embargo, which had come into effect at the beginning of the month, would last until the company was "satisfied that [the garment's] association with the Proud Boys ha[d] ended."[92] Fred Perry asserted that the violent "neo-fascist" group had "appropriated" its shirt and "subverted our Laurel Wreath to their own ends."[93] The appeal of this particular polo shirt and colorway to the Proud Boys is unclear. One commentator has suggested that it resembles the color and design of the ceremonial flag used by Adolf Hitler, the far-right dictator of Germany between 1933 and 1945, which featured his party's black swastika symbol encircled by a gold laurel wreath.[94]

The decision of a fashion brand to rescind a product because of an appropriative act that it deemed distasteful is unusual, not least because of the negligible global influence of the Proud Boys, and Fred Perry's response was widely discussed in the anglophone press.[95] But precedents exist. In 2005, Burberry withdrew its checkered caps from sale and reduced production of its nova check.[96] The meaning of the appropriative acts involving these brands was different, but in both cases the motivation was predicated upon similar social and political factors, as marginal groups used popular and identifiable fashion motifs to gain a coherent visual identity and wider public

IMAGE 14 A person (right) mimics a member of the Proud Boys (centre), who wears a black and yellow Fred Perry polo shirt. Nashville, Tennessee, August 2023.
Source: Getty images.

notice.[97] At a time of heightened class awareness in Britain following the resounding electoral success of the Labour Party, which formed a majority government in 1997 for the first time since 1971, Burberry was concerned about the popularity of one of its most identifiable designs among consumers, derisively termed "chav," which "sat outside of [its] expected demographic."[98] In the case of Fred Perry, appropriation of one of its polo shirts was considered evidence of the increased polarization of politics, particularly in the United States during the presidency of Donald Trump, who infamously appeared to condone the Proud Boys in a televised debate. When asked if he would denounce white supremacists, and with the Proud Boys cited as an example of one such faction, the president addressed the group directly, telling them to "stand back and stand by."[99] These words gave the alt-right all-male group an immediate international profile and platform. The hashtag #whitesupremacy began to trend on X (then, Twitter) and variations of the president's remarks featured in memes.[100] T-shirts with the phrase "Proud Boys standing by" were also sold.[101] While the Proud Boys' appropriation of a Fred Perry garment was notable and newsworthy during a period of acute social and political anguish, their act has greater significance because appropriation forms an important part of the clothing brand's history. This includes a lengthier association with right-leaning groups whose visual aesthetic has incorporated the laurel wreath motif.

Fred Perry created his eponymous brand in the 1940s. A self-taught tennis player, he won consecutive Wimbledon championships between 1934 and 1936. Harnessing his accomplishment and associated celebrity, Perry adapted—appropriated—the laurel wreath associated with the championships to form part of his brand's visual identity. The polo shirt, which remains one of its most identifiable products, was launched in 1952.[102] A conventional narrative avers that the garment, initially only available in white, was considered smart—practically, because of its cut; figuratively, because of its association with a working-class man who gained professional and social esteem—and affordable. Consequently, the Fred Perry polo shirt came to be associated with respectability. This explanation is used by commentators to explain why the garment proved popular among minoritized communities and was paired with styles from subcultural groups and the dress of immigrants, notably those from Jamaica and Barbados.[103] The introduction of multiple colorways during the 1950s increased the shirt's appeal among soccer fans, who were able to wear a garment that closely resembled their team's strip. The association between Fred Perry and soccer was notable in areas of northern metropolitan England where clubs were preponderant. In these areas, where communities were predominantly white, connotations of the polo shirt began to shift during the late 1960s. The garment was increasingly associated with hard mods, or skinheads, who were being recruited to a newly formed nationalist party.[104] During the 1970s, under the premiership of Conservative prime minister

Margaret Thatcher, the connection between Fred Perry polo shirts and fringe right-wing groups increased. By the 1980s, a similar linkage was being made in the United States during the presidency of Republican Ronald Reagan.[105]

An association between Fred Perry and right-leaning groups created a potential for public relations problems, but prior to 2020 the brand had never intervened to restrict the supply of its clothing to consumers. In their statement denouncing the Proud Boys, Fred Perry referenced previous subcultural groups that had "adopted" its garments as a "uniform," and their pride in this "lineage":

> The Fred Perry shirt is a piece of British subcultural uniform, adopted by various groups of people who recognize their own values in what it stands for. We are proud of its lineage and what the Laurel Wreath has represented for over 65 years: inclusivity, diversity and independence.[106]

The history alluded to here is selective because it focuses on a period when appropriation of the brand was less politically charged, but it establishes that Fred Perry is not fundamentally opposed to appropriation. In fact, when appropriation is aligned to the brand's self-proclaimed values, it is considered to enrich its history and contemporary relevance.

Consequently, when Fred Perry responded to the Proud Boys' appropriation in 2020, their objection was about a specific usage of their garments that challenged how it perceived itself, and how it wanted to be perceived by its consumers. While it might be argued that this flexibility aligns with Richard Rogers' assertion that appropriative acts constitute culture, because managing them makes more sense than trying to mount an assault against them, it is apparent that Fred Perry's attitude to appropriation is not pragmatic. In accepting some appropriative acts, which it incorporates into its history, and in downplaying or dismissing other acts that it occludes from its history, the brand appears to presume that it owns, and can therefore control—certainly influence—the connotations and use of its garments at, and even beyond, the point of purchase. Regardless of whether Fred Perry, or any fashion brand, can exert such an authority, explanation of the Proud Boys' adoption of the Black/Yellow/Yellow twin tipped (polo) shirt further demonstrates that attitudes to appropriation are socially constructed and contingent. Journalists were inclined to explain the Proud Boys' adoption of the polo shirt as a difference of degree, linking it to earlier appropriations of the brand by right-wing groups. By contrast, Fred Perry's statement presented the Proud Boys' adoption as a difference of kind by carefully framing histories of appropriation to repudiate links with the organization and to emphasize its own "inclusivity, diversity and independence."[107]

Episode 6. Copyright Infringement: Adidas AG *vs* Thom Browne Inc., 2021–2023

In the episodes above power has emerged as a decisive factor that shapes the form and fallout of discussions about appropriation in fashion. This can be a racial power, a gendered power, a sexual power; it can combine elements of all of these. This final episode considers economic power and focuses on the copyright infringement case that was brought against American luxury brand Thom Browne Inc. by German sportswear brand Adidas AG. Cases of this nature are rare because of the financial and reputational costs that can be incurred, and because legal protection for fashion designs is scant. Nonetheless, Adidas has used legal action to protect its visual identity on previous occasions against other clothing labels, including Abercrombie, Juicy Couture, Marc Jacobs, Ralph Lauren, and Sketchers.

The grievance between Adidas and Thom Browne was longstanding. In 2006, Adidas first challenged Thom Browne's use of a three-stripe motif on its garments because of the resemblance to its

IMAGE 15 Fashion designer Thom Browne (centre) arrives at court in New York City for his case with Adidas, January 2023.
Source: Getty images.

own trademarked three-stripe logo, which it had first used in 1952. The brand's leisurewear has made use of the same logo since 1967.[108] In response to Adidas' concerns, Thom Browne amended their motif to include a fourth stripe, which debuted in the brand's spring 2009 collection.[109] Adidas appeared to accept this change; they certainly did not contest it. Between 2015 and 2017 they pursued legal cases against Marc Jacobs and Juicy Couture for infringement of its three-stripe logo but did not renew their challenge against Thom Browne. The situation changed in 2018 when the luxury brand applied to trademark its three-stripe red, white, and blue Grosgrain Signature logo.[110] In 2021, Adidas formerly filed infringement of copyright and dilution of earnings charges against Thom Browne for the use of banded stripes on its garments. Adidas claimed $867,225 (£711,244) in licensing fees and over $7 million in lost profits.[111] Summing up his case in court, Robert Maldonado, Browne's lead counsel, asserted that "Adidas does not own stripes."[112] The jury concurred, and in January 2023 Adidas lost their case.

Maldonado's plucky retort is undoubtedly correct. No person or brand can lay claim to owning stripes.[113] Nonetheless, a battle of and for stripes is how the case was regarded by several anglophone commentators. In the UK, *The Guardian* ran a story under the headline, "Adidas loses four stripes court battle with designer Thom Browne."[114] The headline of a *Vogue Business* article was more assertive: "Adidas vs. Thom Browne: Who owns the stripe?"[115] Language that invokes ideas of battles and references possession, as much the appearance of Thom Browne wearing the striped garments of his eponymous brand in court (along with some of his supporters in the gallery), suggests the case, for all of its legal formalities, was a symbolic performance. My contention is that the lawsuit is most usefully interpreted as an attempt by Adidas to harness the secondary meaning of its trademarked logo—its widespread recognition, even goodwill—in tandem with the authority of law, to demonstrate the brand's commercial and cultural significance, or power. Here, there are parallels with Fred Perry's actions against the Proud Boys. This explanation may seem lofty, but Adidas has filed ninety lawsuits since 2008 in protection of the twenty-four federal trademarks that it has for the three-stripe logo. This is an average of six cases per year between 2008 and 2023. Moreover, Adidas had no obvious gain against Thom Browne. Financial damages were sought, but Maldonado claimed to be "perplexed" why Adidas, a sportswear brand, would pursue legal action against a luxury brand that was so distinctive. Adidas did claim that Browne's company was moving into the sportswear market, but Maldonado asserted that "he is a high-end, luxury fashion designer, not a designer selling functional activewear."[116] A similar distinction can be claimed of Marc Jacobs, whom Adidas accused of seeking to confuse and "deceive consumers" in the law suit it issued against the brand in 2015.[117]

As law student Caroline Hardig remarks, Adidas' case against Browne demonstrates the extensive resources that it has at its disposal to maintain its market position. This occasion, those that came before it and those that may well follow, amount to a performance of power that can be staged by a wealthy "western" brand. Reflecting on his court triumph, Browne expressed hope that it would encourage independent brands to assert their rights against other and larger corporations. So much so that he felt that "it was important to fight and tell my story."[118] The elephant in the room, which Browne did not acknowledge, is that his company's revenues of $360 million (€330 million) are a far cry from what many independent fashion brands earn. Moreover, few owners of independent brands have access to tell their story through the global anglophone media. By way of comparison, Moïse (Moses) Turahirwa's Moshions was projecting a revenue of $1.5 million for 2023 and several news stories relating to the brand are unretrievable in the UK, presumably because they originate in Rwanda.[119] In this sense, Maldonado's tongue-in-cheek comment about the owning of stripes exposes not only the "western"-centric nature of the legal case, which is probably only feasible for a "western" company to undertake, but of its reporting and understanding, which focused on possession.

It is also noteworthy how analysis of the case's ruling occurred within law-based blogs. This level of concern and scrutiny rarely happens when the appropriative act under review is cultural. Fundamentally, this episode asserts that property is conflated with whiteness, as legal scholar Cheryl Harris asserts and, following her, how discussions of appropriation reinforce "western" and white ascendancy as Pham asserts.[120]

Reflections

The six episodes of appropriation considered are intentionally diverse to demonstrate the prevalence of the phenomenon within the fashion industry, the multiplicity of contrasting opinions that exist about it, and the challenge of aligning public and academic discourses to

IMAGE 16 A model wearing an ensemble from Jean Paul Gaultier's 'Chic Rabbis' collection, 1993.

comprehensively understand the issues involved. Five observations by way of summary can be made. First, the episodes demonstrate that there is a separation between academic discourses on appropriation and public discourses on appropriation, which are framed by the writing of fashion journalists. The latter typically galvanize socialized "western" values and perpetuate negative cultural stereotypes about non-"western" cultures and people. Second, while it is possible to define concepts relating to appropriation, as academics have done, the reality is that multiple views of the phenomenon exist concurrently and there are markedly different assumptions about its acceptability. This point aligns with scholars Denise Nicole Green's and Susan

Kaiser's query about who is interested in appropriation and their assertion, in response to an analysis of Jean Paul Gaultier's Chic Rabbis collection of 1993, that the fashion industry "is not interested in the debate around the ethics of appropriation" and is more concerned with "saleability."[121] The episodes considered here suggest that fashion journalists and fashion insiders consider appropriation to be a tolerable axiom of the fashion industry. By contrast, consumers and academics whose proximity to the industry is further removed, generally appear critical. Third, and linked, much of the reporting about appropriation that appears in the media focuses on the immediate costs and benefits of the appropriative act.[122] It generally does not consider the longer-term causes or implications of such acts, unless these have tangible and consequential actions for the fashion industry. This point is evidenced by the media's spasmodic reporting on the work of diversity officers employed by fashion brands. Between 2018 and 2020, some of the largest "western" fashion conglomerates and brands hired a diversity for the first time—H&M, Nike (2018); Burberry, Chanel, Gucci (2019); LVMH (2020).[123] In most cases the appointment formed part of a package of strategies to wrest the company from a public relations quagmire that appeared to expose a lack of inclusivity and cultural awareness. Nonetheless, few commentators considered the significance of so many "western" fashion brands hiring diversity officers within a short chronological period. Since then, news reports have tended to document the hire and departure of these employees, which typically follows after an equally small time span, with similar brevity.[124] Finally, and to provide a link to the final chapter's reflections on where we go next, the complexities of appropriation, in both act and analysis, are perhaps best explained through the concept of transculturation, which makes appropriation a defining part of culture.

3
WHERE ARE WE GOING?

At the beginning of this book I invoked the words of former British prime minister Winston Churchill to convey some sense of the knottiness of appropriation; its cultural, emotional, intellectual, legal, and linguistic complexities. I also quoted cultural scholar Minh-Ha T. Pham, who has expressed dismay at the reductive and repetitive debates that tend to characterize public and academic discourse about appropriation. The cursory and incomplete discussions about the phenomenon are, I think, chiefly a consequence of our inability or unwillingness to grasp the messiness of what appropriation is.

A focus on products and possession, on immediate acts and attributions of guilt, seems sensible and logical because it appears to deliver results. After a transgression is exposed, the perpetrators are identified, held to account in the court of public opinion; perhaps also the anteroom of academic analysis, and willingly or forcibly undertake an act of contrition. Consequently, we can reassure ourselves that a form of justice has been meted out; that a figurative balance has been restored. The six episodes of appropriation analyzed, not least the existing scholarship and public discussions that I have drawn upon, demonstrate that this perception is inadequate. Multiple forms of appropriation within the fashion industry occur concurrently and continuously, effecting people's cultures, histories, labor, memories; fundamentally, their rights to self-expression. People's responses to these appropriative acts are as diverse as they are multiple, shaped by the platforms and shifting circumstances in which they are voiced and interpreted. These plural and unstable conceptions of appropriation are unlikely to find easy resolution and restitution through a singular process, however well established and rehearsed.

To understand appropriation, from the positives to problems that it creates, we need to be prepared to accept and embrace its messiness, and its inevitably.

Above all, as I asserted in the introduction, I think we need to place appropriation within a larger chronological frame that permits historical reflection. A diachronic perspective, which considers a longer chronology, would enable us to understand how the conception and conduct of appropriation that we grapple with today is framed by "western" prisms of thought—modernity, coloniality, and race—that were defined in the crucible of empire during the eighteenth and nineteenth centuries. If we do not fully acknowledge this history and recognize how appropriative acts and the assumptions that underpin them perpetuate essentialist "western" thought, it is doubtful, given how mundane, unassuming—even neutral—they can appear to be, that the phenomenon will ever be clearly comprehended and, where necessary, challenged.

To be specific, five observations, which frame the calls for action in the book's final chapter, can be made:

1 The complexity of appropriation should be acknowledged. Appropriation is a multifaceted phenomenon. It has different causes and consequences, and these give rise to divergent points of view. The singular and seemingly separable terms of appropriation, cultural appropriation, cultural appreciation, and so on, render a topic defined by its shades of grey monochrome. The deceptive simplicity of having different terms for appropriative acts enforces disciplinary separation with the consequence that incidents of appropriation tend to be analyzed as though they constitute differences of kind. Separate searches for causality, consequences, and cures are therefore pursued. If the complexity of appropriation were acknowledged, with myriad forms of the phenomenon

analyzed together, appropriation and cultural appropriation, for the most part, would be acknowledged as differences of degree and not kind. Artificial classifactory divisions obscure how appropriative acts are predicated on the same "western"-centric thinking and perpetuate the same assumptions based on (mis)understandings of modernity, colonialism, and race. At the very least, it should be recognized that the cultural ethics and labor ethics of appropriation, which tend to be treated separately, have similar historical and ideological origins.

2 Analysis of appropriation should be placed within a larger and more complicated chronological and cultural frame. The dynamic role of history, which informs attitudes and behaviors in the present and perpetuates "western" essentialist thinking that was crystallized during the eighteenth and nineteenth centuries through the experiences of "western" industrialization and colonialism, provides the socialized justification for appropriation. It is the source of what Ayanna Thompson has termed "white innocence." This cannot be critiqued and effectively challenged if the reporting and analysis of appropriative acts in fashion continues to be synchronic, focused on specific time periods and events without consideration of historical antecedents. Interrogation of these acts ought to be diachronic, and incorporate broader chronological, cultural, and geographical perspectives. This should form part of a wider commitment to critically interrogate the role of fashion in the communication of the stories we tell about ourselves and our global cultures.

3 There should be a commitment to unlearning the legacies of colonialism. While this may sound abstract, idealistic, to unlearn is to challenge the orthodoxy, the apparent obviousness, of "western" thinking and the institutions through which they are conveyed—the school, university,

museum, library, archive, and the media.[1] Ariella Aïsha Azoulay, professor of modern culture and media, advocates the practice of potential history. This requires us to conceive of the present through an avoidance of concepts and constructs that were defined in the crucible of empire. This is not an exercise in counterfactual history, but a recognition that the experiences of empire established trajectories of thought and behavior upon existing frameworks that we can resurrect. She explains that "[un]learning is returning to the initial refusal of dispossession and the world out of which it emerged and bringing that moment into our present rather than looking for future, better anti-imperialisms. Scholarly critiques of imperialism's drive toward progress have, in this way, not altered the default temporal givens of imperial ontology."[2]

In the case of fashion, there is an imperative, first, to understand how the contemporary industry continues to perpetuate colonial thought that makes appropriation permissible.[3] Within fashion education the four-point manifesto outlined by fashion scholar Ben Barry, which envisages "an overhaul of our entire curricula and culture," can spur the required discussions and actions.[4]

4 Academic and public discourses about appropriation should be unified. The models and theories that scholars use to understand and unravel the riddle of appropriation need to be accessible to consumers—who seem most likely to call out designers and brands for appropriative acts—and to fashion journalists—whose commentaries tend to sustain the marginalizing attitudes they ostensibly seek to overturn. This is only feasible if academics become more publicly involved, and at an earlier stage, in appropriation discussions. My remarks here are framed by Ben Barry's and Alison Matthews David's suggestion that scholars should readily embrace the fact that fashion studies "ruptures traditional academic silos because

fashion is a social, cultural, economic, and aesthetic force" and has enormous potential to connect with other disciplines and fields, as well as interest groups and industry sectors beyond the academy.[5]

5 The inevitability of appropriation should be acknowledged. Appropriative acts are a fundamental part of human culture. Richard Rogers' concept of transculturation, which moves appropriation from a culture's periphery to its center, best explains the importance, inevitability, and deeply embedded place of appropriation in human lives. Consequently, attitudes and theoretical models that denounce appropriation and seek to stop it are misplaced. By acknowledging appropriation as a social fact, efforts can more purposefully focus on how the phenomenon can become more equitable.

A CALL TO ACTION

Drawing upon previous chapters, this final section of the book includes actions and provocations to support a fuller awareness and avoidance of appropriation within fashion (listed in alphabetical order).

Acknowledge

Fashion designs take inspiration from multiple sources, which require respect and full acknowledgment.

Ask

People's beliefs, cultures, ideas, labor, and materials should never be taken. Their use by others should always be requested.

Awareness

Appropriation is sustained by ignorance of global cultures. Greater awareness of the diversity of the world's cultures is needed.

Caring

Caring can be applied throughout the fashion system, for humans, nature, and the environment, as well as for clothes.

Connection

Confronting appropriation requires academics, consumers, and industry to come together through sustained and critical discourse. Greater efforts are required to bring these groups together.

Consumer citizens

As citizens, consumers have a responsibility to call out appropriation when it occurs and to assert their expectations of the fashion industry by lobbying large corporations and government bodies toward greater accountability and sensitivity for the world's global cultures.

De-centralize

Appropriation reflects an imbalance within global power relations that privilege the "west." Confronting appropriation requires "western" practices and behaviors to be de-centered.

Fashion—reimagined

Fashion must be reimagined as a practice, not just as the purchase of prescribed commodities.

History

The fashion industry needs to acknowledge more directly and consistently the role of history as a dynamic agent in people's lives that informs their values and behaviors.

Language

The words used to label, explain, and debate appropriation are anglophone. There should be acknowledgment of how this frames attitudes and actions to this topic, and greater efforts to center non-English and non-"western" voices.

Local

Value the local, economic, and political power inside communities, and the importance to people of a sense of identity rooted in culture and belief systems, all of which impact clothes.

Meaning

Recognize that the origins of a garment, and what this represents for their creators, makers, and communities, contributes its meaning as a cultural object.

Privilege

Privilege sustains appropriation. Everyone within the fashion system must question and challenge their assumptions and biases.

Race

Appropriation is facilitated by systemic racism. The excuse of ignorance or not knowing better is no excuse.

Redefinition

The fashion system and "big F" fashion does not have to dominate how fashion is defined.

Systems change

The fashion system must change to acknowledge its responsibilities to people and the planet, not just to increase the economic profit of the few.

Time

Confronting appropriation means disrupting fashion time, which emphasizes forward motion and linearity. More time needs to be spent reflecting on what is, and what has been.

Value

Awareness and avoidance of appropriation requires people to recognize the emotional, intellectual, and physical value involved in the conception and creation of garments.

NOTES

Introduction

1 Susan Ratcliffe, ed., *Oxford Essential Quotations*, 6th edition (Oxford: Oxford University Press, 2018).

2 This is the premise of arguments made by Thorstein Veblen, *The Theory of the Leisure Class*, ed. Martha Banta (Oxford: Oxford University Press, [1899] 2007) and Georg Simmel, "Fashion," *Georg Simmel on Individuality and Social Forms*, ed. Donald N. Levine (Chicago and London: The University of Chicago Press, [1903] 1971), 294–323.

3 Minh-Ha T. Pham, *Why We Can't Have Nice Things: Social Media's Influence of Fashion, Ethics, and Property* (Durham: Duke University Press, 2022), 13.

4 André Leon Talley, *The Chiffon Trenches: A Memoir* (London: 4th Estate, 2020), 144.

5 Benjamin Linley Wild, "Critical Reflections on Cultural Appropriation, Race and the Role of Fancy Dress Costume," *Critical Studies in Fashion and Beauty*, 11:2 (2020), 156; James O. Young and Conrad G. Brunk, eds., *The Ethics of Cultural Appropriation* (London: Blackwell, 2009), 9.

6 Khémaïs Ben Lakhdar, *L'appropriation Culturelle: Histoire, domination et création: aux origins d'un pillage occidental* (Paris: Éditions Stock, 2024).

7 Yuniya Kawamura and Jung-Whan Marc de Jong, *Cultural Appropriation in Fashion and Entertainment* (London: Bloomsbury, 2022), 49–101.

8 See below, 25–27.

9 Denise Nicole Green and Susan B. Kaiser, "Taking Offense: A Discussion of Fashion, Appropriation, and Cultural Insensitivity," *The Dangers of Fashion: Towards Ethical and Sustainable Solutions*, eds. Sara B. Marcketti and Elena E. Karpova (London: Bloomsbury, 2020), 148.

10 Kawamura and Marc de Jong, *Cultural Appropriation*, 94; Pham, *Why We Can't Have Nice Things*, 24–5, 99–123.

11 www.faceandrace.org.

12 Kimberly Jenkins, "About," https://artissolomon.com.

13 Yuniya Kawamura, *Fashion-ology: An Introduction to Fashion Studies* (Oxford: Berg, 2005), 1.

14 Linda Welters and Abby Lillethun, *Fashion History: A Global View* (London: Bloomsbury, 2018), 4.

15 Anon., "History," https://www.kcl.ac.uk/about/history. Accessed: October 2023.

16 Angela Jansen, "Fashion and the Phantasmagoria of Modernity: An Introduction to Decolonial Fashion Discourse", *Fashion Theory*, 24: 2 (2020), 1–22.

17 Khémaïs Ben Lakhdar proposes a similar, but different "trinity of modernity": capitalism, colonialism, and industrialization. *L'appropriation Culturelle: Histoire, domination et création: aux origins d'un pillage occidental* (Paris: Éditions Stock, 2024), 135.

18 Elizabeth Wilson, *Adorned in Dreams: Fashion and Modernity* (London: I.B. Tauris, [1985] 2003), 63.

19 Caroline Evans and Alessandra Vaccari, "Time in Fashion: An Introductory Essay," *Time in Fashion: Industrial, Antilinear and Uchronic Temporalities*, eds. Caroline Evans and Alessandra Vaccari (London: Bloomsbury, 2020), 12–13.

20 Evans and Vaccari, "Time in Fashion, 13.

21 Benjamin L. Wild, *Hang-Ups: Reflections on the Causes and Consequences of Fashion's "Western"-Centrism* (London: Bloomsbury, 2024), 10–15.

22 Discussed by Daniel Miller, "The Little Black Dress is the Solution. But What's the Problem?" *Elusive Consumption*, eds. K. Ekstrom and H. Brembeck (Oxford: Berg, 2004), 113–27.

23 Daniel Miller, *Modernity: An Ethnographic Approach* (London: Routledge, 1994), 58–81.

24 Wild, *Hang-Ups*, 3–4.

25 Gilles Lipovetsky, *The Empire of Fashion: Dressing Modern Democracy*, translated by Catherine Porter (Princeton and Oxford: Princeton University Press, [1987] 1994), 18.

26 Miller, *Modernity*, 58–81.

27 Norbert Elias, *The Society of Individuals*, ed. Michael Schröter, translated by Edmund Jephcott (Oxford: Basil Blackwell [1987] 1991), 129.

28 J. Hills Miller, "Narrative," *Critical Terms for Literary Study*, 2nd edition, eds. Frank Lentricchia and Thomas McLaughlin (Chicago and London: The University of Chicago Press, 1995), 70.

29 Alison Slater, Susan Atkin and Elizabeth Kealy-Morris, "Introduction," *Memories of Dress: Recollections of Material Identities*, eds. Alison Slater, Susan Atkin, and Elizabeth Kealy-Morris (London: Bloomsbury, 2023), 14–19.

30 Simon Reynolds, *Retromania: Pop Culture's Addiction to Its Own Past* (London: Faber and Faber, 2011), xii.

31 Reynolds, *Retromania*, 189.

32 Ibid., 195.

33 Ibid., 194.

34 Catherine Hall, "Introduction: Thinking the Postcolonial, Thinking the Empire," *Cultures of Empire: Colonizers in Britain and the Empire in the Nineteenth and Twentieth Centuries. A Reader*, ed. Catherine Hall (Manchester: Manchester University Press, 2000), 7.

35 Wild, *Hang-Ups*, 97.

36 Jayne Elizabeth Lewis, *Mary Queen of Scots: Romance and Nation* (London: Routledge, 1998), 78.

37 Wild, *Hang-Ups*.

38 David Graeber and David Wengrove, *The Dawn of Everything: A New History of Humanity* (London: Penguin, 2021), 495.

39 Wild, *Hang-Ups*, 183.

40 Pham, *Why We Can't Have Nice Things*, 41.

41 Cheryl L. Harris, "Whiteness as Property," *Harvard Law Review*, 106:8 (1993). 1721.

42 Ibid., 1735–6.

43 Minh-Ha T. Pham, *Why We Can't Have Nice Things*, 72.

44 Ibid., 59–60.

45 Ibid., 61–5.

46 Meredith Oyen, "'Artless Dealing': The First Year of Trump's Relations with China," *The Journal of American-East Asian Relations*, 25:2 (2018), 113–37.

47 Serkan Delice, “Where Is Living Labour in Fashion and Cultural Appropriation Debates?,” *Fashion’s Transnational Inequalities: Socio-political, Economic, and Environmental*, eds. Anna-Mari Almila and Serkan Delice (London and New York: Routledge, 2023), 49–50.

48 Minh-Ha T. Pham, “Fashion’s Cultural Appropriation Debate: Pointless,” *The Atlantic* (May 15, 2014).

49 Delice, “living labour,” 54.

50 Pham, “Fashion’s Cultural Appropriation Debate.”

51 Ibid.

52 Young and Brunk, eds., *Ethics of Cultural Appropriation*, 9.

Chapter 1

1 Khémaïs Ben Lakhdar, *L’appropriation Culturelle: Histoire, domination et création: aux origins d’un pillage occidental* (Paris: Éditions Stock, 2024), 9–12.

2 Further definitions for cultural-exchange, -borrowing’, -inspiration, -hybridity, -insensitivity are provided by Denise Nicole Green and Susan B. Kaiser, “Taking Offense: A Discussion of Fashion, Appropriation, and Cultural Insensitivity,” *The Dangers of Fashion: Towards Ethical and Sustainable Solutions*, eds. Sara B. Marcketti and Elena E. Karpova (London: Bloomsbury, 2020), 144–7.

3 “Appropriation, n.,” *OED Online* (Oxford University Press).

4 Ibid.

5 Pamela Fletcher and Anne Helmreich, eds., *The Rise of the Modern Art Market in London, 1850–1939* (Manchester: Manchester University Press, 2011); Thomas M. Bayer and John R. Page, *The Development of the Art Market in England: Money as Muse, 1730–1900* (London: Pickering & Chatto, 2011).

6 Minh-Ha T. Pham, *Why We Can’t Have Nice Things: Social Media’s Influence of Fashion, Ethics, and Property* (Durham: Duke University Press, 2022), 10.

7 Benjamin Linley Wild, “Cultural Appropriation in Fashion, Dress, and Appearance,” *Bloomsbury Fashion Central* (London: Bloomsbury Academic, 2015).

8 "Cultural appropriation, n.," *OED Online* (Oxford University Press).

9 Ibid.

10 Ibid.

11 "Cultural appropriation," Google Books Ngram viewer.

12 Object 2018.1. "Paul Poiret, Black beaded silk evening dress, Autumn/Winter 1921–1922," Unpicking Couture, Manchester Art Gallery, July 21, 2023–January 12, 2025.

13 Ben Lakhdar, *L'appropriation Culturelle*, 52.

14 Laird Borrelli-Pearson, "Charting the Impact of the Ballets Russes—from Yves Saint Laurent to Grimes," *Vogue* (3 November 2015). https://www.vogue.com/article/ballets-russes-yves-saint-laurent-grimes. Accessed: June 2024.

15 Benjamin L. Wild, *Hang-Ups: Reflections on the Causes and Consequences of Fashion's "Western"-Centrism* (London: Bloomsbury, 2024), 122–7.

16 Joanne P. Sharp, *Geographies of Postcolonialism* (London: Sage, 2009), 73–6.

17 Mike Thelwall, Olga Goriunova, Farida Vis, Simon Falkner, Anne Burns, Jim Aulich, Amalia Mas-Bleda, Emma Stuart, and Francesco D'Orazio, "Chatting Through Pictures? A Classification of Images Tweeted in One Week in the UK and USA," *Journal of the Association for Information Science and Technology*, 67:11 (2016), 2575.

18 See above, 8.

19 See above, 10–11.

20 Serkan Delice, "Critiques of Appropriation and Transnational Labor Ethics," *Fashion Theory*, 26:4 (2022), 486.

21 Ben Lakhdar, *L'appropriation Culturelle*, 14.

22 "Cultural appreciation," Google Books Ngram viewer.

23 Minh-Ha T. Pham, "Racial Plagiarism and Fashion," *QED*, 4:3 (2017), 68.

24 Ibid., 73. See below, 25–26.

25 Ayanna Thompson, *Blackface* (London: Bloomsbury, 2021), 5–18.

26 "Culture, n.," *OED Online* (Oxford University Press).

27 Ibid.

28 Kathleen Wilson, *The Island Race: Englishness, Empire and Gender in the Eighteenth Century* (London: Routledge, 2003), 195; Rudi C. Bleys, *The Geography of Perversion: Male-to-Male Sexual Behaviour outside the West and the Ethnographic Imagination 1750–1918* (London: Cassell, 1996), 165; Jessica Hinchy, "The Sexual Politics of Imperial Expansion: Eunuchs and Indirect Colonial Rule in Mid-Nineteenth-Century North India," *Gender, Imperialism and Global Exchanges*, ed. Stephan F. Miescher, Michelle Mitchell, and Naoko Shibusawa (Chichester: John Wiley & Sons, 2015), 33.

29 Raymond Williams, *Culture and Society 1780-1950* (London: Penguin [1958] 2017), 1–6.

30 "Culture," Google Books Ngram viewer.

31 Norimitsu Onishi and Constant Méheut, "Heating Up Culture Wars, France to Scour Universities for Ideas that 'Corrupt Society,'" *The New York Times* (February 18, 2020). https://www.nytimes.com/2021/02/18/world/europe/france-universities-culture-wars.html. Accessed: February 2020.

32 James O. Young and Conrad G. Brunk, eds., *The Ethics of Cultural Appropriation* (London: Blackwell, 2009), 3.

33 Bruce Ziff and Pratima V. Rao, eds., *Borrowed Power: Essays on Cultural Appropriation* (New Jersey: Rutgers University Press, 1997), 2.

34 Martin Puchner, *Culture: A New World History* (London: Ithaka Press, 2023), xx, 278.

35 Young and Brunk, *The Ethics of Cultural Appropriation*, 2–4.

36 Puchner, *Culture*, x–xii.

37 Ibid., 279–80.

38 Homi K. Bhabha, *The Location of Culture* (London: Routledge, 1994), ix–x.

39 Bhabha, *The Location of Culture*, 2.

40 Ibid., 2–3.

41 Ibid., 51, 94.

42 Ibid., 10.

43 Angela Jansen, introductory text for the online course "Decolonial Fashion Discourses & Praxis" that was organized by the Research Collective for Decoloniality and Fashion in 2023.

44 Rosie Findlay and Johannes Reponen, "Introduction," *Insights on Fashion Journalism*, eds. Rosie Findlay and Johannes Reponen (London: Bloomsbury, 2023), 1.

45 Benjamin Wild, *Hang-Ups: Reflections of the Causes and Consequences of Fashion's "Western"-Centrism* (London: Bloomsbury, 2024), 158, 161.

46 Martha E. Sanchez, "Caliban: The New Latin-American Protagonist of the Tempest," *Diacritics*, 6:1 (1976), 54–61. I am grateful to Regina Root for their insight.

47 See above, 11.

48 Minh-Ha T. Pham, "Fashion's Cultural Appropriation Debate: Pointless," *The Atlantic* (15 May 2014).

49 Pham, "Fashion's Cultural Appropriation Debate."

50 Ibid.

51 Ben Lakhdar, *L'appropriation Culturelle*, 122.

52 Pham, "Racial Plagiarism and Fashion," 68–9, 72.

53 Ibid., 70.

54 Ibid., 71.

55 Ibid., 69.

56 Ibid., 74–5.

57 Ibid., 75.

58 Ibid., 76.

59 Ibid., 76–7.

60 Ibid., 77.

61 Delice, "Transnational Labor Ethics," 486–7.

62 Ibid., 486.

63 Serkan Delice, "Where Is Living Labour in Fashion and Cultural Appropriation Debates?," *Fashion's Transnational Inequalities: Socio-political, Economic, and Environmental*, eds. Anna-Mari Almila and Serkan Delice (London and New York: Routledge, 2023), 47.

64 Delice, "Where Is Living Labour."

65 Ibid., 57, 58, 60; Delice, "Transnational Labor Ethics," 478.

66 Ibid.

67 Ibid., 479.

68 Delice, "Where Is Living Labour," 61.

69 Yuniya Kawamura and Jung-Whan Marc de Jong, *Cultural Appropriation in Fashion and Entertainment* (London: Bloomsbury, 2022), 1–2.

70 Kawamura and de Jong, *Cultural Appropriation*, 64.

71 Ibid.

72 Ibid.

73 Ibid., 65.

74 Ibid., 70, 76, 77.

75 Ibid., 93.

76 Ibid., 173, 175.

77 Ibid., 175.

78 Ibid.

79 Ibid., 175.

80 Toyne V. Erekosima and Joanne B. Eicher, "The Aesthetics of Men's Dress of The Kalabari of Nigeria," *The Visible Self: Global Perspectives on Dress, Culture, and Society*, ed. Joanne B. Eicher and Sandra Lee Evenson, fourth edition (London: Bloomsbury, 2015), 352.

81 John E. Vollmer, "Cultural Authentication in Dress," *Berg Encyclopedia of World Dress and Fashion: Global Perspectives*, eds. Joanne B. Eicher and Phyllis G. Tortora (Oxford: Berg, 2010), 69.

82 See above, 23.

83 Erekosima and Eicher, "The Aesthetics of Men's Dress of The Kalabari of Nigeria," 349.

84 Ibid., 351.

85 Ibid., 350; Kawamura and de Marc Jong, *Cultural Appropriation in Fashion and Entertainment*, 173–4.

86 Vollmer, "Cultural Authentication in Dress," 69.

87 Kawamura and Marc de Jong, *Cultural Appropriation in Fashion and Entertainment*, 174.

88 Richard A. Rogers, "From Cultural Exchange to Transculturation: A Review and Reconceptualization of Cultural Appropriation," *Communication Theory* 16 (2006), 475–6.

89 Rogers, "From Cultural Exchange to Transculturation," 475.

90 Ibid., 474.
91 Ibid., 477.
92 Ibid., 478.
93 Ibid.
94 Ibid., 478–9.
95 Ibid., 479.
96 Ibid., 480–3.
97 Ibid., 481.
98 Ibid., 485.
99 Ibid., 483.
100 Ibid., 486.
101 Ibid., 486–7.
102 Ibid., 491.
103 Ibid.
104 Ibid.
105 Ibid., 492.
106 Ibid., 499.

Chapter 2

1 Minh-Ha T. Pham, “Fashion’s Cultural Appropriation Debate: Pointless,” *The Atlantic* (May 15, 2014).

2 Minh-Ha T. Pham, *Why We Can’t Have Nice Things: Social Media’s Influence of Fashion, Ethics, and Property* (Durham: Duke University Press, 2022), 10, 25.

3 Rosie Findlay and Johannes Reponen, “Introduction,” *Insights on Fashion Journalism*, eds. Rosie Findlay and Johannes Reponen (London: Routledge, 2022), 1.

4 Findlay and Reponen, “Introduction,” 4–5.

5 For example, see Yuniya Kawamura and Jung-Whan Marc de Jong, *Cultural Appropriation in Fashion and Entertainment* (London: Bloomsbury, 2022), 67–8, 79; Paul Jobling, Philippa Nesbitt, Angelene Wong, *Fashion, Identity, Image* (London: Bloomsbury, 2022), 105–37.

6 Morwenna Ferrier, "Gucci Withdraws $890 Jumper after Blackface Backlash," *The Guardian* (February 7, 2019).

7 Ayanna Thompson, *Blackface* (London: Bloomsbury 2021), 5–6.

8 Dapper Dan Instagram @dapperdanharlem (February 10, 2019).

9 Ibid.

10 Luisa Zargani, "Gucci Launches Initiatives to Foster Cultural Diversity and Awareness," *WWD* (February 15, 2021).

11 Luisa Zargani, "EXCLUSIVE: Gucci's Marco Bizzarri on Learning Amid Blackface Accusations," *WWD* (February 12, 2019); Alyssa Vingan Klein, "Internal Memo from Gucci CEO Shows He's Taking the Blackface Scandal Very, Very Seriously," *Fashionista* (February 11, 2019); Anon., "Alessando Michele Breaks His Silence About Gucci's Blackface Scandal," *Fashionista* (February 12, 2019).

12 Channing Hargrove, "Gucci Issues Internal Statement About Blackface Sweater," *Refinery29* (February 13, 2019), https://www.refinery29.com/en-gb/gucci-blackface-wool-sweater-apology. Accessed: December 2023.

13 Anon., "Alessando Michele."

14 Benjamin L. Wild, *Hang-Ups: Reflections on the Causes and Consequences of Fashion's "Western"-Centrism* (London: Bloomsbury, 2024), 159.

15 Thompson, *Blackface*, 5–15.

16 Amy Held, "Gucci Apologizes And Removes Sweater Following 'Blackface' Backlash," *NPR* (February 7, 2019).

17 Ibid.

18 For a fuller analysis of Cyborg, see Wild, *Hang-Ups*, 66–71.

19 Alice Norris and Lorenzo Cantoni, *Digital Fashion Communication: An (inter)cultural Perspective* (Leiden and Boston: Brill, 2022), 86–7.

20 Sarah Mower, "Gucci: Fall 2018 Ready-to-Wear," *Vogue* (February 21, 2021).

21 Jobling, Nesbitt, Wong, *Fashion, Identity, Image*, 116.

22 Tyler McCall, "Gucci Out-Guccis Itself for Fall 2018," *Fashionista* (February 21, 2018).

23 Mower, "Gucci."

24 Tahmina Begum, "Gucci Criticised for Cultural Appropriation on a Global Scale," *HuffPost* (February 22, 2018).

25 Jobling, Nesbitt, Wong, *Fashion, Identity, Image*, 119, 125.

26 Ibid., 128–36.

27 See Chapter 1, 33–34.

28 Jobling, Nesbitt, Wong, *Fashion, Identity, Image*, 116.

29 Mower, "Gucci."

30 See Chapter 1, 25–26.

31 Jenni Avins, "Mexico's Female Rodeo Stars Inspired Dior's Latest Collection," *Quartz* (May 26, 2018).

32 Erica Tempesta, "'This Is Ignorant and Gross!' Dior Is SLAMMED Online for Casting Jennifer Lawrence in a New Ad Campaign That Claims to Celebrate MEXICAN Heritage," *The Daily Mail* (November 21, 2018).

33 Alexander Fury, "The Diorodeo: Horses, Corsets and Female Liberation at Dior Cruise," *Another* (May 27, 2018).

34 Tempesta, "This Is Ignorant and Gross!."

35 Ibid.

36 Sally Singer, "Christian Dior: Resort 2019," *Vogue* (May 25, 2018).

37 Fury, "The Diorodeo."

38 Ibid.

39 Dominique Muret, "Dior Hosts a Chic Mexican-Inspired Rodeo in Chantilly," *Fashion Network* (May 26, 2018).

40 Muret, "Mexican-Inspired Rodeo in Chantilly."

41 Virginia Marie Betz, "On the History of the Mexican Charro: A Review Essay," *Journal of the Southwest*, 37:3 (1995), 510–17.

42 Fury, "The Diorodeo."

43 Ibid.

44 Ibid.

45 Muret, "Mexican-Inspired Rodeo in Chantilly."

46 Ibid.

47 Ibid.

48 Ibid.

49 Ibid.

50 Ibid.

51 See Chapter 1, 28.

52 Muret, "Mexican-Inspired Rodeo in Chantilly."

53 Fury, "The Diorodeo."

54 Yuniya Kawamura, *Fashion-ology: An Introduction to Fashion Studies* (Oxford: Berg, 2005), 1.

55 Jennifer Ayres, "Inspiration or Prototype? Appropriation and Exploitation in the Fashion Industry," *Fashion, Style and Popular Culture*, 4:2 (2017), 151–65.

56 Moshions *Intsinzi* "Trouser Suit," Victoria & Albert Museum online collection; Moses Turahirwa, "Moshions," *Africa Fashion* (London: V&A Publishing, 2022), 159.

57 Turahirwa, "Moshions," 158.

58 Moses K. Gahigi, "Moshions, Bespoke Kigali Label on Global Stage," *The East African* (February 21, 2020).

59 Gahigi, "Moshions, Bespoke Kigali Label on Global Stage."

60 Ibid.

61 I am grateful to Ken Kweku Nimo for his helpful insights and leads, although the conclusions reached are my own.

62 Michele D. Wagner, "Rwanda and Burundi," Joanne B. Eicher and Doran H. Ross, eds. *Berg Encyclopedia of World Dress and Fashion: Africa* (Oxford: Berg, 2010), 465.

63 Mackenzie Moon Ryan, *African Apparel: Threaded Transformations across the 20th Century* (New York: Scale Arts Publishers, Inc., 2020), 38–9.

64 Ryan, *African Apparel*, 38.

65 See Chapter 1, 29–30.

66 See Chapter 1, 33–34.

67 Oliver Grady, "Pose Star Billy Porter: Did I Ever Think I'd Be This Successful? No, Because I'm Gay," *The Sunday Times* (October 17, 2021).

68 Orin Carlin, "Harry Styles: the Ultimate Rundown of the Singer's Most Stylish Moments," *Hello! Fashion* (February 3, 2023).

69 Marlene Lenthang, "Harry Styles Opens Up About His Sexuality and Addresses Queerbaiting Accusations," *NBC News* (October 23, 2022).

70 Jireh Deng, "Harry Styles Isn't the Leader of a Fashion Revolution, but Neither Is Billy Porter," *NPR* (October 20, 2021).

71 Deng, "Harry Styles."

72 Ibid.

73 Daniel Rodgers, "Just How Revolutionary Is Harry Styles' Vogue Cover," *Dazed* (November 19, 2020).

74 Deng, "Harry Styles."

75 Ibid.

76 Ariel Sobel, "Is It Ever Okay to Try On Queerness?" *Pride* (June 27, 2017).

77 Sobel, "Is It Ever Okay."

78 Ibid.

79 Ibid.

80 For example, see Anny Shaw, "Lesbian, Gay, Bisexual and Transgender Artists Warn Against the Appropriation of Queer Imagery by Straight Artists," *The Art Newspaper* (October 1, 2014).

81 See above, 7–8.

82 Tsione Wolde-Michael, "A Brief History of Voguing," *National Museum of African American History and Culture* (no date). https://nmaahc.si.edu/explore/stories/brief-history-voguing. Accessed: August 2023.

83 Nicky Papilaja, "Cultural Appropriation in RuPaul's Drag Race," *Truth or Tea* (no date); Lillian Dam Bracia, "Weighing in on Cultural Appropriation and Drag," *Indie* (August 30, 2013); Portia B., "How Do We Fix Appropriation in the Drag Community?," *Gal—dem* (June 3, 2018).

84 Bracia, "Weighing in on Cultural Appropriation and Drag."

85 Mikhail Bakhtin, *Rabelais and his World*, translated by Hélène Iswolsky (Bloomington & Indianapolis: Indiana University Press, [1965] 1984).

86 Benjamin Linley Wild, "Critical Reflections on Cultural Appropriation, Race and the Role of Fancy Dress Costume," *Critical Studies in Fashion & Beauty*, 11:2 (2020), 160–1.

87 Wolde-Michael, "A Brief History of Voguing."

88 Portia B., "How Do We Fix Appropriation in the Drag Community?"

89 See Chapter 1, 25–26.

90 Frantz Fanon, *The Wretched of the Earth*, translated by Constance Farrington (New York: Grove Press, 1963), 209–10.

91 Serkan Delice, “Where Is Living Labour in Fashion and Cultural Appropriation Debates?,” *Fashion’s Transnational Inequalities: Socio-political, Economic, and Environmental*, eds. Anna-Mari Almila and Serkan Delice (London and New York: Routledge, 2023), 47.

92 Anon., “Proud Boys Statement,” Fred Perry website (September 24, 2020).

93 Anon., “Proud Boys Statement.”

94 Elizabeth Segran, “Why the Far Right Proud Boys Co-Opted These Polo Shirts,” *Fast Company* (October 7, 2020).

95 Hayley Spencer, “A Brief History of the Fred Perry Polo Shirt and Its Complicated Connection to Hate Groups,” *The Independent* (September 29, 2020).

96 Daniel Rodgers, “It’s Been 20 Years Since Danniella Westbrook Was Labelled ‘Chavtastic’ for Wearing Full-Look Burberry, and Yet the Nova Check Remains a Weathervane for the UK’s Turbulent Relationship with Class,” *Dazed* (May 26, 2022).

97 Rodgers, “It’s Been 20 Years.”

98 Ibid.

99 Derek Hawkins, Cleve R. Wootson Jr. and Craig Timberg, “Trump’s ‘Stand By’ Remark Puts the Proud Boys in the Spotlight,” *The Washington Post* (September 30, 2020).

100 Hawkins, Wootson and Timberg, “Trump’s ‘Stand By’ Remark.”

101 Ibid.

102 Nosheen Iqbal, “Fashion … or Fascist? The Long Tussle Over That Fred Perry Logo,” *The Guardian* (October 4, 2020).

103 Spencer, “Fred Perry polo shirt.”

104 Ibid.

105 Ibid.

106 Anon., “Proud Boys Statement.”

107 Ibid.

108 Lauren Cochrane, "Adidas Loses Four Stripes Court Battle with Designer Thom Browne," *The Guardian* (January 13, 2023); Dan Howarth, "Adidas Sues Marc Jacobs for 'Tarnishing' Three-Stripe Motif," *Dezeen* (April 11, 2015).

109 Angela Wei, "Everything You Need To Know About the Adidas vs. Thom Browne Trademark Case [Updated]," *Fashionista* (January 12, 2023).

110 Wei, "Adidas vs. Thom Browne."

111 Cochrane, "Four Stripes Court Battle."

112 Wei, "Adidas vs. Thom Browne."

113 Anne Gallagher, "Thom Browne Trial Win Shows Why Luxury Brands Should Understand the Scope Of Trademark Protection," *The Global Legal Post* (March 2, 2023).

114 Cochrane, "Four Stripes Court Battle."

115 Madeleine Schulz, "Adidas vs. Thom Browne: Who Owns the Stripe?," *Vogue Business* (January 6, 2023).

116 Gallagher, "Thom Browne Trial Win"; Caroline Hardig, "Adidas 'Does Not Own Stripes,'" *University of Cincinnati Law Review*, 91 (March 14, 2023).

117 Howarth, "Adidas Sues Marc Jacobs."

118 Cochrane, "Four Stripes Court Battle."

119 Gahigi, "Moshions."

120 See Chapter 1, 25–26.

121 Denise Nicole Green and Susan B. Kaiser, "Taking Offense: A Discussion of Fashion, Appropriation, and Cultural Insensitivity," *The Dangers of Fashion: Towards Ethical and Sustainable Solutions*, eds. Sara B. Marcketti and Elena E. Karpova (London: Bloomsbury, 2020), 151.

122 Green and Kaiser, "Taking Offense," 153.

123 Jasmin Malik Chua, "Why Fashion Needs Chief Diversity Officers," *Business of Fashion* (November 21, 2019).

124 For example, Cara Salpini, "Nike Loses Third Diversity Officer in 2 Years," *Retail Dive* (November 15, 2022); Lucas Manfredi, "Nike's First-Ever Chief Diversity and Inclusion Officer Departs," *Fox Business* (July 27, 2020).

Chapter 3

1 Angela Jansen, "Fashion and the Phantasmagoria of Modernity: An Introduction to Decolonial Fashion Discourse," *Fashion Theory* (2020), 8.

2 Ariella Aïsha Azoulay, *Potential History: Unlearning Imperialism* (London: Verso, 2019), 21.

3 Benjamin Linley Wild, *Hang-Ups: Reflections on the Causes and Consequences of Fashion's "Western"-Centrism* (London: Bloomsbury, 2024).

4 Ben Barry, "How to Transform Fashion Education: A Manifesto for Equity, Inclusion and Decolonization," *International Journal of Fashion Studies*, 8:1 (2021), 124.

5 Ben Barry and Alison Matthews David, "A Fashion Studies Manifesto: Toward an (Inter)disciplinary Field," special issue of *Fashion Studies*, 1:1 (2023), 1–23.

SELECTED FURTHER READING

Azoulay, Ariella Aïsha, *Potential History: Unlearning Imperialism* (London: Verso, 2019).

Ayres, Jennifer, “Inspiration or Prototype? Appropriation and Exploitation in the Fashion Industry,” *Fashion, Style and Popular Culture*, 4:2 (2017), 151–65.

B., Portia, “How Do We Fix Appropriation in the Drag Community?,” *Gal—dem* (June 3, 2018).

Barry, Ben, “How to Transform Fashion Education: A Manifesto for Equity, Inclusion and Decolonization,” *International Journal of Fashion Studies*, 8:1 (2021), 123–30.

Barry, Ben and David, Alison Matthews, “A Fashion Studies Manifesto: Toward an (Inter)disciplinary Field,” special issue of *Fashion Studies*, 1:1 (2023), 1–23.

Ben Lakhdar, Khémaïs, *L’appropriation Culturelle: Histoire, domination et création: aux origins d’un pillage occidental* (Paris: Éditions Stock, 2024).

Bhabha, Homi K., *The Location of Culture* (London: Routledge, 1994).

Bleys, Rudi C., *The Geography of Perversion: Male-to-Male Sexual Behaviour outside the West and the Ethnographic Imagination 1750–1918* (London: Cassell, 1996).

Bracia, Lillian Dam, “Weighing in on Cultural Appropriation and Drag,” *Indie* (August 30, 2013).

Chua, Jasmin Malik, “Why Fashion Needs Chief Diversity Officers,” *Business of Fashion* (November 21, 2019).

Delice, Serkan, “Critiques of Appropriation and Transnational Labor Ethics,” *Fashion Theory*, 26:4 (2022), 475–91.

Delice, Serkan, “Where Is Living Labour in Fashion and Cultural Appropriation Debates?,” *Fashion’s Transnational Inequalities: Socio-political, Economic, and Environmental*, eds. Anna-Mari Almila and Serkan Delice (London and New York: Routledge, 2023), 47–64.

Erekosima, Toyne V. and Eicher, Joanne B., "The Aesthetics of Men's Dress of The Kalabari of Nigeria," *The Visible Self: Global Perspectives on Dress, Culture, and Society*, ed. Joanne B. Eicher and Sandra Lee Evenson, fourth edition (London: Bloomsbury, 2015), 349–61.

Evans, Caroline and Vaccari, Alessandra, "Time in Fashion: An Introductory Essay," *Time in Fashion: Industrial, Antilinear and Uchronic Temporalities*, eds. Caroline Evans and Alessandra Vaccari (London: Bloomsbury, 2020), 3–10.

Fanon, Frantz, *The Wretched of the Earth*, translated by Constance Farrington (New York: Grove Press, 1963).

Findlay, Rosie and Reponen, Johannes, "Introduction," *Insights on Fashion Journalism*, eds. Rosie Findlay and Johannes Reponen (London: Bloomsbury, 2023), 1–12.

Fletcher, Pamela and Helmreich, Anne, eds., *The Rise of the Modern Art Market in London, 1850–1939* (Manchester: Manchester University Press), 2011.

Graeber, David and Wengrove, David, *The Dawn of Everything: A New History of Humanity* (London: Penguin, 2021).

Green, Denise Nicole and Kaiser, Susan B., "Taking Offense: A Discussion of Fashion, Appropriation, and Cultural Insensitivity," *The Dangers of Fashion: Towards Ethical and Sustainable Solutions*, eds. Sara B. Marcketti and Elena E. Karpova (London: Bloomsbury, 2020), 143–60.

Hall, Catherine, "Introduction: Thinking the Postcolonial, Thinking the Empire," *Cultures of Empire: Colonizers in Britain and the Empire in the Nineteenth and Twentieth Centuries. A Reader*, ed. Catherine Hall (Manchester: Manchester University Press, 2000), 1–33.

Harris, Cheryl L., "Whiteness as Property," *Harvard Law Review*, 106:8 (1993), 1707–91.

Held, Amy, "Gucci Apologizes And Removes Sweater Following 'Blackface' Backlash," *NPR* (February 7, 2019).

Hills Miller, J., "Narrative," *Critical Terms for Literary Study*, second edition, eds. Frank Lentricchia and Thomas McLaughlin (Chicago and London: The University of Chicago Press, 1995), 66–79.

Jansen, Angela, "Fashion and the Phantasmagoria of Modernity: An Introduction to Decolonial Fashion Discourse," *Fashion Theory* (2020), 1–22.

Jobling, Paul, Nesbitt, Philippa, Wong, Angelene, *Fashion, Identity, Image* (London: Bloomsbury, 2022).

Kawamura, Yuniya, *Fashion-ology: An Introduction to Fashion Studies* (Oxford: Berg, 2005).

Kawamura, Yuniya and Marc de Jong, Jung-Whan, *Cultural Appropriation in Fashion and Entertainment* (London: Bloomsbury, 2022).

Lipovetsky, Gilles, *The Empire of Fashion: Dressing Modern Democracy*, translated by Catherine Porter (Princeton and Oxford: Princeton University Press, [1987] 1994).

Pham, Minh-Ha T., *Why We Can't Have Nice Things: Social Media's Influence of Fashion, Ethics, and Property* (Durham: Duke University Press, 2022).

Pham, Minh-Ha T., "Racial Plagiarism and Fashion," *QED*, 4:3 (2017), 67–80.

Pham, Minh-Ha T., "Fashion's Cultural Appropriation Debate: Pointless," *The Atlantic* (May 15, 2014).

Puchner, Martin, *Culture: A New World History* (London: Ithaka Press, 2023).

Reynolds, Simon, *Retromania: Pop Culture's Addiction to Its Own Past* (London: Faber & Faber, 2011).

Rogers, Richard A., "From Cultural Exchange to Transculturation: A Review and Reconceptualization of Cultural Appropriation," *Communication Theory*, 16:4 (2006), 474–503.

Ryan, Mackenzie Moon, *African Apparel: Threaded Transformations across the 20th Century* (New York: Scale Arts Publishers, Inc., 2020).

Sharp, Joanne P., *Geographies of Postcolonialism* (London: Sage, 2009).

Shaw, Anny, "Lesbian, Gay, Bisexual and Transgender Artists Warn Against the Appropriation of Queer Imagery by Straight Artists," *The Art Newspaper* (October 1, 2014).

Sobel, Ariel, "Is It Ever Okay to Try on Queerness?," *Pride* (June 27, 2017).

Thompson, Ayanna, *Blackface* (London: Bloomsbury, 2021).

Turahirwa, Moses, "Moshions," *Africa Fashion* (London: V&A Publishing, 2022), 158–9.

Veblen, Thorstein, *The Theory of the Leisure Class*, ed. Martha Banta (Oxford: Oxford University Press, [1899] 2007).

Vollmer, John E., "Cultural Authentication in Dress," *Berg Encyclopedia of World Dress and Fashion: Global Perspectives*, eds. Joanne B. Eicher and Phyllis G. Tortora (Oxford: Berg, 2010), 69–76.

Wagner, Michele D., "Rwanda and Burundi," Joanne B. Eicher and Doran H. Ross, eds. *Berg Encyclopedia of World Dress and Fashion: Africa* (Oxford: Berg, 2010), 461–70.

Welters, Linda and Lillethun, Abby, *Fashion History: A Global View* (London: Bloomsbury, 2018).

Wild, Benjamin Linley, *Hang-Ups: Reflections on the Causes and Consequences of Fashion's "Western"-Centrism* (London: Bloomsbury, 2024).

Wild, Benjamin Linley, "Cultural Appropriation in Fashion, Dress, and Appearance," *Bloomsbury Fashion Central* (London: Bloomsbury, 2015).

Wild, Benjamin Linley, "Critical Reflections on Cultural Appropriation, Race and the Role of Fancy Dress Costume," *Critical Studies in Fashion & Beauty*, 11:2 (2020), 153–73.

Williams, Raymond, *Culture and Society 1780–1950* (London: Penguin [1958] 2017).

Young, James O. and Brunk, Conrad G., eds., *The Ethics of Cultural Appropriation* (London: Blackwell, 2009).

Ziff, Bruce and Rao, Pratima V., eds., *Borrowed Power: Essays on Cultural Appropriation* (New Brunswick: Rutgers University Press, 1997).

INDEX